Be *Filled* with the *Spirit*

Doyle Jones

TATE PUBLISHING, LLC

This book is designed to provide accurate and authoritative information with regard to the subject matter covered. This information is given with the understanding that neither the author nor Tate Publishing, LLC is engaged in rendering legal, professional advice. Since the details of your situation are fact dependent, you should additionally seek the services of a competent professional.

ISBN: 1–5988610–1-8

Table of Contents

Foreword 7

Preface 11

The Meaning of Being Filled With the Spirit 13

The Spirit Filled Life is Not For Everybody–Just Believers . 27

Being Filled With the Spirit Is Not Difficult 33

Steps To Being Filled With the Spirit 49

Be Being Filled With the Spirit 63

"Be Filled With the Spirit"–Option or Command? 71

How to Help People to Be Filled With the Spirit. 79

Why All Believers Should Be Filled With the Spirit 93

Evidences of Pentecost 111

Frequently Asked Questions About Speaking in Tongues . 121

Foreword

One hour can change your Christian life!

That's about how long it will take to read this straightforward presentation of Bible principles and patterns. In these few pages, Dr. Doyle Jones gives simple instruction and practical application of biblical truths to help you receive the Baptism in the Holy Spirit (and to help others receive). But this empowering experience will usher you into a new dimension of Christian life and service.

During the past 100 years, millions of Christians have received their personal Pentecost. This 21st Century finds Pentecostalism, including classic Pentecostal and charismatic congregations, as perhaps the fastest growing religious movement in the world.

Dr. Jones belongs to a worldwide fellowship which exists to give continuing emphasis to evangelism, worship, and discipleship in the New Testament apostolic pattern by teaching and encouraging believers to be baptized in the Spirit. He has aggressively pursued this mandate for more than four decades as an evangelist, missionary, pastor, university professor and missions director. In more than 25 nations on four continents, and in more than 500 congregations in the United States, he has presented the life-giving, life-building message of Jesus Christ as Savior, Healer, Spirit Baptizer and returning King. He has helped found and finance 36 churches and schools around the world. In addition to his university classes and extensive local church ministry, he continues to circle the global each year leading students in planting and cultivating new churches.

The truths you are about to explore are both practical and proven. Dr. Jones moves Pentecost, Spirit Baptism, and speaking in tongues from the realm of religious theory to Great Commission reality.

More than an addendum to salvation, a religious upgrade, or an attainment for the super spiritual, Baptism in the Spirit is an injunction for Christian purpose. The Baptism in the Holy Spirit is not so much about you and what you receive as about impacting your family, your neighbors, your community, and your world with the transforming message of Jesus.

God's provision for every believer, this baptism brings enablement and power for taking the Good News to all the world. In the process, not as the purpose but as a product, you will discover the Holy Spirit enhancing and enriching every area of your own life and service.

Mel Surface
District Christian Education Director
North Texas Assemblies of God

Preface

This book is an outgrowth of many years of helping people to be baptized in the Holy Spirit. The bulk of the material was written several years ago following an evangelistic meeting one night. I came in from a tremendous service in which several had been filled with the Spirit. Without premeditation, I sat down at the table in our travel trailer and began to write about being baptized in the Holy Spirit. Normally, writing requires a lot of thought and deliberation on my part, but that night I wrote effortlessly and as rapidly as I could write.

The material that I compiled that night has helped countless numbers of individuals receive the precious infilling in the Holy Spirit. The last few years it has been my privilege to share this information in many different seminars all over the world. It is my sincere desire that many others will be helped in the future through reading the instructions written in this book.

The approach chosen has been to write in understandable language in order to help the layman receive the infilling of the Holy Spirit. The book is not a *deep* theological treatment, as I explain in chapter one, *but a practical approach to theological truth*. Those seeking to be baptized in the Holy Spirit should prayerfully concentrate on the first four chapters before proceeding to the other chapters.

Chapter One

The Meaning of Being Filled
With the Spirit

Mary was firm in her belief of what being "filled with the Spirit" means. She lingered after each service in order to express her views.

I had preached that when God fills someone with the Holy Spirit, he or she will speak with other tongues. After the service, she cornered me with questions.

"How can you say that? How can you say that only those who have spoken with other tongues have been filled with the Holy Spirit?"

She insisted she knew she had been filled with the Spirit because she had recently gone forward at a youth meeting and received the infilling by faith. "I did not speak in tongues," she argued, "but I felt the presence of God all over me. Ever since that time I have had a great desire to witness and tell others about Jesus."

Mary added "I do not have anything against

speaking in tongues, but I just do not think that it is necessary to do that when a person is filled with the Spirit."

Many people are like Mary. They may cite some great spiritual experience after they were saved which they believe was being filled with the Spirit. Often they take a theological position that some may speak with tongues and some may not when baptized in the Spirit.

Sometimes these people believe that speaking in tongues really is not for Christians today. They may even hold that those who speak in tongues are deceived by their own emotions and do not have a biblically sound experience. Still others believe that Christians are baptized in the Holy Spirit at the moment of their conversion.

The purpose of this book is not to prove the validity and necessity of speaking in tongues. Many others have addressed this issue in depth.[1] My objective is to help hungry believers receive the Baptism in the Holy Spirit.

However, since uncertainty about tongues poses a hindrance for many, a brief look at some of the biblical basics concerning tongues should be helpful.

Two Different Purposes of Speaking in Tongues

One of the first objections Mary raised was the question of the Apostle Paul in 1 Corinthians 12:30, "Do all speak with tongues?" (NKJV) She inferred that speaking in tongues is not for everyone.

I explained that the Bible sets forth two distinct functions of speaking in tongues. First, it is the initial physical evidence of the Baptism in the Holy Spirit as demonstrated in the Book of Acts. It continues in the life of the Spirit-filled believer as a prayer privilege and means of spiritual growth.

Paul dealt with a second function in his writings to the Corinthian church. He lists and gives instructions for nine manifestations or gifts God has included in the worship services and ministries of His Church. In this context, Paul asks, "Do all speak with tongues?" He also asks, "Do all interpret?"

Not all Christians are used in these gifts, though every Spirit-filled believer can be. Paul instructs, " . . . earnestly desire the best gifts" (1 Cor. 12:31a, NKJV).

Acts focuses on people receiving the Holy Spirit while 1 Corinthians 12–14 gives guidelines for exercising a public gift of tongues. In this instance, an individual gives an utterance in tongues to be followed by an interpretation which will bless and edify the whole congregation. While everyone speaks in tongues at his/her Baptism in the Spirit, not everyone is to exercise the gift of tongues to be interpreted as part of public worship.

Paul was writing to people who already spoke in tongues, who had already experienced the Book of Acts infilling, who already practiced prayer in the Spirit, and some of whom were now being used in the worship services in a gift ministry.

Speaking in tongues builds up the individual (1 Cor. 14:2–5, TAB). It would seem to contradict God's nature as "no respecter of persons" (Acts 10:34, KJV) to give some believers a private means for spiritual development not available to all. But the gift of tongues in the church service must be interpreted for the good of all.

Paul makes clear that no spiritual gift is meaningful without love (1 Cor. 13:1). He insists that Spirit-filled believers demonstrate concern for others in all they say or do. The manifestation of tongues mentioned in 1 Corinthians may be the same in nature and essence as tongues in Acts, but they differ in purpose.

Mary and I reviewed three accounts in Acts saying recipients of the Holy Spirit Baptism spoke in tongues. We also looked at two instances in which individuals were baptized in the Holy Spirit but tongues were not mentioned.

Instances of Speaking in Tongues in Acts

The New Testament first records speaking in tongues in Acts 2 when God initially poured out His Spirit on the disciples on the Jewish Day of Pentecost.[2] Obeying the Lord's command to "stay in the city of Jerusalem until you are endued with power from on high" and with His promise of Baptism in the Holy Spirit (Luke 24:49 and Acts 1:4, 5), the disciples waited and worshiped. And on the Day of Pentecost, " . . . they were all filled with the Holy Spirit and began to speak with other tongues, as the Spirit gave them utterance" (Acts 2:4, NKJV). This Scripture clearly declares that when the Holy Spirit came on the 120 present (Acts 1:15), they all began to speak with other tongues.

Later, when Peter's preaching of the resurrected Christ moved the multitude to cry out, "Men and brethren what shall we do?" (Acts 2:37, NKJV),

Peter told them to repent and be baptized. Then, he said, "You shall receive the gift of the Holy Spirit" (Acts 2:38). (Notice he said "gift" not "gifts.")

The second example of tongues speaking happened when Peter shared the message of Christ with the household of the Gentile captain, Cornelius. Luke declared,

> While Peter was still speaking these words, the Holy Spirit fell upon all those who heard the Word. And those of the circumcision who believed were astonished, as many as came with Peter, because the gift of the Holy Spirit had been poured out on the Gentiles also. For they heard them speak with tongues and magnify God (Acts 10:44–46, NKJV).

Notice two things here: (1) Verse 45 says that on the Gentiles was poured out the *gift* - not the "gifts" of the Holy Spirit. The Bible here is not speaking of the gifts that Paul was trying to regulate in the Corinthian church, just as Peter was not speaking of those gifts on the day of Pentecost. (2) The text also says that Peter and the Jews that had accompanied him to Cornelius' house knew that these Gentiles had received the infilling of the Spirit *"for they heard them speak with tongues and magnify God."*

The manifestation of tongues was proof enough for Peter and those with him. The Jewish believers instantly recognized that the Gentiles had been filled with the Spirit because they heard them speak with tongues. When they baptized them immediately in water, this important outward symbol signified that the Gentiles were acknowledged as members of the Body of Christ, the Church.

The third specific reference of speaking in tongues details an experience of Paul's:

> . . . Paul having passed through the upper regions came to Ephesus; and finding some disciples, he said to them, "Did you receive the Holy Spirit when you believed?" And they said unto him, "We have not so much as heard whether there is a Holy Spirit . . ." And when Paul had laid hands on them, the Holy Spirit came upon them and they spoke with tongues and prophesied (Acts 19:1–2, 6; NKJV).

Here some Ephesians who were called disciples came into a more excellent knowledge of Jesus

Christ. These men had knowledge of Jesus Christ already. Stanley Horton says,

> Some writers believe these were disciples of John the Baptist. But everywhere else in the Book of Acts where Luke mentions disciples, he always means disciples of Jesus, believers in Jesus, followers of Jesus . . . Though Paul sensed there was something lacking in their experience, he did not question the fact that they were believers. In fact, he recognized they were . . . [3]

They accepted Paul's instructions and were baptized again since their previous baptism was limited to the baptism of John. (Note: These believers were filled with the Spirit after baptism in water. Cornelius and his household were filled before their water baptism. Before or after water baptism, a hungry Christian can be filled now!)

When Paul laid his hands on these believers, the Bible says they spoke in tongues as they were filled. The Ephesians received the same experience as the early church some twenty years previously on the day of Pentecost.

Two Other Instances of Spirit Baptisms

But what about the other two accounts? The first record of people receiving the Holy Spirit which does not include speaking in tongues is Acts 8:14–17.

> Now when the apostles who were at Jerusalem heard that Samaria had received the word of God, they sent Peter and John to them, who, when they had come down, prayed for them that they might receive the Holy Spirit. For as yet He had fallen upon none of them. They had only been baptized in the name of the Lord Jesus. Then they laid hands on them and they received the Holy Ghost (NKJV).

These verses do not specifically state that the people of Samaria spoke with other tongues. But in verse 18, Simon the sorcerer wanted so desperately to have this gift ("Give me also this power") not only for himself but also that he might lay hands on others to receive, that he offered to pay for the gift. Simon evidently witnessed a phenomenon he had never seen. He already had seen miracles (v. 6), demons cast out (v. 7), and tremendous prevailing joy (v. 8). But here was something different. The evidence points to speaking with other tongues as the sign.

It was not necessary for Luke to specify that the Samaritans spoke in tongues in this instance. His audience would have associated speaking in tongues with the account. As Horton indicates,

> Luke often does not explain everything when it is clear elsewhere. For example, he does not mention water baptism every time he tells about people believing or being added to the church, but it is clear that the failure to mention this is not significant.[4]

In this same chapter, Luke mentions that Simon was baptized (Acts 8:13) but it does not say he was baptized in water. The reader would not need that clarification. The context of Luke's writings would be sufficient for any observer to know that Luke meant "baptism in water." In the same way, by studying the rest of the Book of Acts, the reader would know that believers spoke in tongues when receiving the Baptism in the Holy Spirit. Though this context does not specifically mention the phenomenon (speaking in tongues), it was not necessary for Luke to indicate that it happened.

Interestingly, Philip, the evangelist who had brought the Gospel to the Samaritans, was not the one to pray with them to receive the Holy Spirit Baptism. Peter and John, central figures in the early development of the church, followed up on Philip's revival. Peter certainly would have recognized whether or not these new converts had received the same infilling as did the 120 on the day of Pentecost. No doubt he used the same criterion as he did later at Cornelius' house: "For they heard them speak with tongues and magnify God" (Acts 10:46, NKJV).

But Peter's presence was not required to determine if the Samaritans had received the Holy Spirit, for Philip was also full of the Holy Spirit (Acts 6:3–7) and would have known if they had received. Nor did Luke the writer need to explain to his audience the normative experience when he stated that the Samaritans received the Holy Spirit. The principle reason for Peter's presence probably was God's desire to demonstrate to this important leader in the early church that the Samaritans, so despised by the Jews, were to be reached and instructed in the spiritual norms of the Church. The Samaritans were no different than the Jews on the day of Pentecost. Though they had accepted Christ through the preaching of Philip, they still needed the Baptism in the Holy Spirit. Nothing would indicate that their experience differed from anyone else who had received previous to that time.

The other account which implies but does not specifically mention speaking in tongues is found in Acts 9:17–18:

> And Ananias went his way and entered the house and laying his hands on him he said, "Brother Saul, the Lord Jesus, who appeared to you on the road as you came, has sent me that you may receive your sight and be filled with the Holy Spirit." Immediately there fell from his eyes something like scales, and he received his sight at once; and he arose and was baptized (NKJV).

Luke doesn't say Paul spoke with tongues but the Apostle later told the Corinthian church, "I thank my God I speak with tongues more than you all" (1 Cor. 14:18, NKJV). Paul makes this statement in his use of the spiritual gifts. He apparently refers to his private devotions rather than the gift of tongues since he adds, "Yet in the church I would rather speak five words with my understanding, that I may teach others also, than ten thousand words in a tongue" (1 Cor. 14:19, NKJV). He had earlier stated, "I will pray with the spirit and with the understanding" (1 Cor. 14:15, NKJV). Elsewhere Paul spoke of the Holy Spirit helping the believer to intercede with "groanings which cannot be uttered" (Rom. 8:26). Clearly he was a frequent tongue talker. When did he begin? He began when Ananias laid hands on him and he was filled with the Holy Spirit. This would follow the established pattern.

God's Plan for Mary

Mary listened but did not accept my explanation. Individuals choose their beliefs for a variety of reasons and may find it hard to accept a different viewpoint. However, God had a plan for Mary.

One Thursday night she came to the meeting where I delivered a message entitled, "The Times of Refreshing." At the invitation several people rushed forward including, to her own amazement, Mary.

Tears streamed down her cheeks as she argued with the personal worker beside her that she wasn't sure she believed in all of this and wasn't certain why she had come to the front. When I went over to her, I was certain that a power greater than she had experienced previously had brought her to the front. I said, "Mary, raise your hands toward heaven." Sobbing, she replied, "But I'm not sure I believe . . ." I interrupted her, "Raise your hands, Mary, in the name of the Lord." She raised her hands and when I laid my hands upon her she started speaking with other tongues. She was filled with the Holy Spirit! She lost an argument but she gained a glorious experience!

Mary had a hungry heart, and hungry, honest hearts are filled when they reach out to God, even when they don't fully understand all the details.

Chapter Two

The Spirit Filled Life is Not For Everybody - Just Believers

Two drunks sat in a beer joint indulging in their favorite pastime. Between gulps one drunk said to the other, "What do you think about this speaking in tongues?" The other answered, "It's of the devil." But the first drunk quickly replied, "Oh, no. It couldn't be. If it was, you and I would have it."

He had a point! Unbelievers are not candidates for the Baptism in the Holy Spirit. In fact, Paul says that "the natural man does not receive the things of the Spirit of God, for they are foolishness to him; nor can he know them because they are spiritually discerned" (1 Cor. 2:14, NKJV).

Two Prerequisites for Receiving

But being filled with the Holy Spirit is not far away from anyone if he or she will fulfill only two prerequisites for receiving: Be saved and be spiritually hungry. The first step, naturally, is conversion.

Conversion and the Baptism in the Spirit

This brings up the question, "Doesn't everyone receive the Holy Spirit at conversion?" Yes, everyone receives the Holy Spirit at conversion, but not the Baptism in the Holy Spirit. Many scriptures confirm that no one can be saved without the agency of the Holy Spirit. Paul declares, "If any man have not the Spirit of Christ, he is none of His" (Rom. 8:9, KJV). The Holy Spirit gives spiritual life to the Christian (vs. 10–11). Paul said, "God hath sent forth the Spirit of His Son into your hearts, crying Abba Father (Gal. 4:6, KJV)." The word *Abba*, Aramaic for "Father," puts emphases on the word "Father" while demonstrating that the Spirit affirms one's position as a child of God. The context of this Scripture reveals how God has taken the believer from the status of slave to the level of sonship. The Spirit has to be present in order to confirm one's position in the family of God.

Other scriptures that bear out the Holy Spirit's participation in conversion are the following: 1 Cor. 12:13, "For by one Spirit are we all baptized into one body" (KJV). Gal. 3:27, "For as many as have been baptized into Christ have put on Christ" (KJV). Rom. 8:16, "The Spirit himself testifies with our spirit that we are God's children" (NIV).

But receiving the third member of the Godhead, the Holy Spirit, at conversion is not the same as being baptized in the Spirit. Peter declared, "Repent and let every one of you be baptized in the name of Jesus Christ for the remission of sins; and you shall receive the gift of the Holy Spirit" (Acts 2:38, NKJV). In Peter's preaching it was repentance first and the gift (not *gifts*) of the Holy Spirit (Baptism in the Spirit) afterwards.

Paul and the Ephesians

Paul said to the Ephesians (Acts 19:2), "Have you received the Holy Ghost since ye believed?" (KJV) But more modern translations read, "Did you receive the Holy Spirit *when* you believed?" (NIV–emphasis mine) This seems to indicate that the reception of the Spirit corresponded to the act of conversion. But noted scholar Stanley Horton responds to those who try to narrowly limit the Greek in this passage. Horton states,

The whole impression of Acts 19:2 is that since these disciples claimed to be believers, the Baptism in the Holy Spirit should have been the next step after believing, though not necessarily separated from it by a long time.[5]

A simple way to demonstrate the difference between salvation and the Holy Spirit Baptism is to compare drinking a glass of water to being baptized or immersed with water. Though one utilizes the identical agent in both functions, the experience is different.

Spiritual Hunger and Baptism in the Spirit

Now, notice the second prerequisite for being filled with the Holy Spirit: spiritual hunger. Jesus declared, "Blessed are they which do hunger and thirst after righteousness for they shall be filled" (Mt. 5:6, KJV). The Lord fills the hungry. He doesn't check the denominational tags to check out church membership. If an individual is born again and has a genuine hunger, he/she is ready for the promised infilling in the Holy Spirit.

I remember when the Lord filled me with the Holy Spirit. I hungered for this experience after my conversion because others had told me how wonderful it was. As a brand new convert at age eleven, I was absolutely thrilled when I accepted Christ. None of my family members (three brothers and two sisters) really served the Lord, though our mother, a widow, believed in God and occasionally took us to a non-Pentecostal church. The Pentecostal church differed dramatically from other church services I had attended, but I was convinced of the reality I had found in Christ. I felt if the Pentecostal experience was for me, then I wanted it.

Oh, how I wanted it! I sought the Baptism in the Holy Spirit every time I came to church, but I just did not know how to receive. My hunger paid off, however. One night the pastor had everyone present come to the front. While I stood praising God, the Spirit of the Lord came over me and suddenly I began to speak in tongues.

Without a deep hunger for all the Lord has for us, we miss great spiritual experiences, including the Baptism in the Holy Spirit. I remember a revival I preached in Louisiana in which one brother had sought the infilling in the Holy Spirit but had not received. He and his family had planned a fishing trip to begin on Friday of the revival. At service time Friday night and with his boat attached to his pickup ready to go, this brother told his family he just had to come to the revival. They changed all their plans at the last minute and came to the meeting. That night this man who had sought the Baptism in the Holy Spirit for years was filled with the Spirit. What made the difference? A hunger for the things of God more than anything else.

Chapter Three

Being Filled With the Spirit is Not Difficult

Some believers who have had difficulty receiving the Baptism in the Holy Spirit are inclined to believe that only a few achieve this remarkable experience. They try ever so hard but every effort seems to end in failure and disappointment. Their minds become battlefields of questions and doubts as they ponder why they cannot receive the Holy Spirit Baptism. They do everything they know to do but with no visible results.

God Wants Us Filled

No matter how hard it may seem to receive the Baptism in the Holy Spirit, God never commands anything He doesn't really intend to be accomplished. He inspired the Apostle Paul to write, "Be filled with the Spirit" (Eph. 5:18, KJV). That alone should encourage you. He *wants* you to be filled.

And if He wants you to be filled, then we know that He will do everything in His power to fill you.

If you have been having difficulty, be encouraged by the fact that He wants you to be filled more than you want to be filled. God is on your side! Praise God! That fact alone ought also to help you identify the source of the trouble. Jesus said, "The thief comes only that he may steal and kill and may destroy. I came that they may have and enjoy life, and have it in abundance—to the full, till it overflows" (Jn. 10:10, TAB - 1965 edition). The context of this verse indicates Satan is "the thief." It contrasts the giver of abundant life with the opposite force who wants to steal, kill and destroy. The devil wants to steal the power of the Spirit from you in any way he can, but Jesus wants you to have joy till it overflows. The greatest source of this joy is the Holy Spirit (Rom. 14:17), and the devil knows it. He will fight you with every fear and doubt he can produce when you start seeking the power of the Spirit.

A list of objections. Because our adversary is so subtle, he often places plausible sounding objections in our minds to prevent us from receiving the Baptism in the Holy Spirit. The following comprises a partial list of objections that Satan puts in a Spirit-filled candidate's mind. I have heard these objections voiced many times.

1. "I know God wants to fill me but for some reason He hasn't seen fit to fill me yet. When He gets ready, I am sure He will." Don't succumb to the illusion that God is waiting for some dramatic moment to fill you with the Holy Spirit. *He has already given the Holy Spirit.* This happened on the day of Pentecost. Spirit Baptism is available to all who are hungry. You decide the issue - God is ready now!

2. "I am not sure that being filled with the Spirit is for me. It's not for everybody, you know." The devil definitely wants you to believe this. On the day of Pentecost, Peter quoted the prophet Joel, "And it shall come to pass in the last days says God that I will pour out of my Spirit on all flesh" (Acts 2:17, NKJV. See Joel 2:28). In the last days God will pour out His Spirit on everyone - irrespective of race, sex, age, class or denomination. That includes you.

In the same sermon in Acts 2:39, Peter declared, "For this great promise is for you and your children— yes, and for all who are far away, *for as many as the Lord our God shall call to Himself*" (Ph, emphasis mine). Forget the idea that God doesn't want to fill you. He definitely has called you to Himself! Acts 10:34 states that "God shows no partiality" (NIV). (Remember that the context of this verse is the conversion of Cornelius' household and the outpouring of the Spirit on that occasion.) Thank God! He is impartial. What He did for Peter, James, and John, He'll do for you!

3. "I guess I'm just not ready. When I get good enough maybe the Lord will fill me." What does it take to get ready? Some people have a catalog of things that they think they must give up in order to receive. But giving up all those things won't earn you the right to receive the Baptism in the Holy Spirit. The Baptism in the Holy Spirit is a gift (Acts 2:38; 8:20; 10:45; 11:17). If you could overcome things in your life without the Holy Spirit, there would be no need to receive the Spirit's power. The Scriptures declare in Acts 1:8, "But ye shall receive power *after* that the Holy Ghost is come upon you" (KJV). Notice that it is *after* or *when* (NIV) and not *before*. John 16:13 clearly indicates that the Holy Spirit will come to guide *after* he has been received.

Misinformed believers trying to help others receive the infilling of the Holy Spirit often fuel the erroneous thought that a hungry believer may not be worthy to be baptized in the Spirit. I have heard well-meaning people tell candidates for the infilling, "There are things you must give up in your life in order to receive the Holy Spirit." But this places the Baptism in the Holy Spirit on the level of merit. You cannot earn the Baptism in the Holy Spirit. No one ever was or ever will be righteous enough to deserve the Baptism in the Holy Spirit.

You will never receive as long as you think that you are not ready. That is faith in reverse or negative faith. *You must believe that you are ready because God made you ready*! Remember, if you are good enough for heaven, you are good enough for the Holy Spirit. Believe that you are ready now to receive.

4. "I've tried so many times before but nothing happened." Every time you seek the Holy Spirit Baptism and are unsuccessful, the devil takes the opportunity to put doubts into your mind. He'll remind you of all the times before and he'll tell you that this time will be no different.

In one revival service, I gave instructions on receiving the Holy Spirit Baptism and then asked those who wanted to receive to come forward. I told them to expect to receive when I laid my hands on them. The first lady I prayed for had sought the Baptism in the Holy Spirit for approximately forty years. Before I laid my hands on her, I asked her if she believed that she would be given words to speak by the Holy Spirit. She tearfully replied, "I just don't know, Brother Jones. I have tried so many times." I replied, "But this time it is going to be different. It is not based on past experience but on what God has for you now. God is going to fill you because of what He has promised." I rebuked the doubt and told her to expect to hear words of another language being given to her. When I laid hands on her, God gave her words and she began speaking another language.

In another service, I prayed for several individuals who received the Baptism in the Holy Spirit. One lady who was filled told me afterward that she was 69 years old and had sought the infilling of the Holy Spirit most of her life before receiving that morning. If she had failed to seek the infilling in that service, she most likely would not have been filled.

5. "Maybe I don't have enough patience to tarry or wait on the Lord as I should." Who said you had to tarry? Only once did Jesus say "tarry" and that was to his disciples. The word *tarry* in the Greek actually means "to sit down and wait." They were to wait until the outpouring of the Spirit on the day of Pentecost. That was not in order for them to get ready by prayer and fasting. It was simply because God, according to His schedule of events, wanted the Spirit to fall on the day of Pentecost, an event exactly fifty days from the Passover. After Pentecost, notice how people received. Luke says they prayed, the place shook, and they were all filled with the Holy Ghost. There is no evidence of tarrying here (Acts 4:31).

In Acts 8:17 Luke states that they laid hands on them and they received the Holy Spirit. Again, this passage does not indicate tarrying between the time of laying on of hands and the time that they received.

Acts 9:17 (Paul's baptism) indicates laying on of hands and receiving without tarrying.

Acts 10:44 shows that the Gentiles received while Peter was just getting wound up in his sermon. No tarrying was necessary.

In Acts 19:6, Paul laid his hands on the Ephesians and they received without tarrying. It does not depend on how long you can hang on that merits the Holy Spirit for you.

However, though tarrying may not be a requirement, it is necessary that the candidate for the infilling of the Spirit be determined to receive. Don't seek the Baptism in the Holy Spirit with concern about time. Make up your mind to spend time in God's presence. In the biblical instances given above, though the filling was instantaneous, in every case those who received were ready because their hearts were prepared. Stay in an attitude of prayer. Walk in God's presence. Don't feel that in order to receive from God it will be necessary to spend time getting ready. Come seeking the Spirit already saturated with God's presence.

6. "I'm afraid I might get in the flesh or the devil might deceive me into saying something false." In the first place, this declaration exemplifies negative faith and you, the candidate, unwittingly set yourself up for failure when asserting that the devil is going to deceive you. It contradicts the very nature of God to think that He would allow you to be tricked into receiving from the devil when you are seeking Him (God).

It is also an unscriptural position. Jesus said,

Is there a father among you who will

offer his son a snake when he asks for a fish, or a scorpion when he asks for an egg? If you, then, bad as you are, know how to give your children what is good for them how much more will the heavenly Father give the Holy Spirit to those who ask him! (Luke 11:11–13, NEB).

If an earthly father knows how to give his child what is good for him, then certainly our heavenly Father will give us what is best for us. If an earthly father would not deceive his child by giving him something other than that which he asked, neither will the heavenly Father allow you to receive anything except that for which you asked.

God will not give you anything false. When you are seeking Jesus for the Baptism in the Holy Spirit and words come to your mind or heart, trust God to not allow the devil to give you something false. The Holy Spirit is impressing you with words of another language. You are receiving what you asked for. Praise God!

7. "I guess I don't have the faith to receive." Anytime you say this you are defeated before you start. *You do have faith*. The Apostle Paul said, " . . .

be honest in your estimate of yourselves, measuring your value by how much faith God has given you" (Rom. 12:3, TLB). In this setting (Ch. 12), Paul speaks of the Christian's responsibilities toward God (1–2) and his responsibilities toward society (3–21). He reminds his readers to realize that God has given faith to the Christian not for his/her own benefit but for the benefit of God and others. Faith must be fed by looking to Jesus (Heb. 12:2) and by reading and hearing the Word (Rom. 1:17).

Hearing the Word prompted the faith of Cornelius and the other Gentiles with him when the Holy Spirit fell on them. Luke wrote, "The Holy Ghost fell on all them *which heard the word*" (Acts 10:44). The Word quickened their faith. Believe what God says. Don't have faith that you won't receive! Repeat the promises of God over and over - not only in your mind but aloud also.

8. "I am distracted when I try to seek for the infilling of the Spirit." Certainly you are. That is Satan's business.

Are you distracted during other prayer times? All prayer demands concentration. Anyone can get into such a rut that he/she prays without thinking about what is being said. One man who was asked to pray over the offering that was about to be received in a church service began his prayer by saying, "Lord, we thank you for this food . . ." The enemy will get you to the point that you are mouthing words of prayer without really thinking about what you are articulating. From all outward appearances, you may seem to be really praying at times but in reality Satan is bringing other distracting thoughts to your mind.

You must withstand the devil while drawing near to God. " . . . Stand firm against the devil; resist him and he will flee from you. Come close to God and He will come close to you." (James 4:7–8, TAB 1965 edition). While contextually this verse does not specifically refer to prayer, it does reveal that our efforts to resist Satan and to draw close to God are rewarded.

Besides its many other components, prayer should involve goals. Keep in mind that you are seeking the Baptism in the Holy Spirit. But keep your mind on Jesus. Keep praising and worshiping Him for He is the Baptizer. Again, realize that God is on your side. He wants you to receive.

9. "Well, you see, I'm just not a very emotional person in the first place, so I don't think this speaking in tongues is for me." Granted, the

Baptism in the Holy Spirit is an emotional experience. It makes one love Jesus more. Anyone who communicates love from deep within will have his or her emotions touched. But the evidence of the Baptism in the Holy Spirit is based on neither emotional reactions nor physical gyrations. Speaking in tongues is the physical evidence. You may or may not have a highly emotional physical reaction.

I was in Africa some years ago preaching a youth camp. A young African received the Baptism in the Holy Spirit with the accompanying evidence of speaking in tongues. After the service he questioned me, "Did I receive the Holy Spirit? I know I spoke in tongues but I didn't fall down." (He had seen a number of the young people get quite emotional and fall down). I told him that it wasn't based on whether he fell down and became quite emotional but whether he spoke in tongues.

How many received on the day of Pentecost? All 120 who were present. Wouldn't it be probable that some in that upper room were not the emotional type? Yet everyone received. Peter did not say, "The promise is unto all of you *except the unemotional*." Who said that emotional reactions were the evidence of speaking in tongues? You may receive the Holy

Spirit very quietly in a manner quite in keeping with your nature. On the other hand, you may react in a very unexpected manner, but you will be so excited about receiving the Holy Spirit that it doesn't matter. For example, Bro. Green, a man from my home church, was a very quiet-natured man and seldom said much. When God filled him with the Holy Spirit, he ran all over the church.

It might be a huge mistake to absolutely declare what you will not do. In one of our meetings, a lady who had been associated with the Pentecostal experience all of her life but who had never received the promised Holy Spirit Baptism made some declarations about how she would not react. This lady had personally known one of the early leaders of the Pentecostal movement in this century and had entertained him in her home. But for some reason, she had not been able to receive. One night during the revival, I went over to pray for her but nothing happened. I rebuked any doubt present and started praying for her in other tongues. As she raised her hands and began to praise God, tears began to stream down her face and she started speaking in a beautiful language. Later she testified that she had always stated that she knew that she would never receive if someone was standing over her, jabbering in tongues, talking to her, and laying hands on her. She was a very quiet individual and felt that the only way she could be filled would be quietly. She discovered that one cannot put God into a straitjacket. God decides how He will fill an individual. It doesn't matter how He does it, just so He does it.

10. "People praying loudly around me get on my nerves. Why do they have to scream?" Some individuals are distracted by others praying for them. Zealous individuals sometimes hinder the candidate by giving confusing instructions or by the sheer volume of their prayers. But, you don't have to receive with people praying around you. You may receive at home, in your car, or on the job.

A mechanic in one of my revivals shut his garage door, went into the bathroom and received the Holy Spirit. He testified that night, "Every time I passed the bathroom today, I started speaking in tongues."

A missionary from a denomination that did not teach the *glossolalia* experience (*glossolalia* is a non-biblical term coined to denote tongues speaking) said in a public service I attended that he got so hungry for God that he had to find a place where he could seek God privately. That place proved to be the ditch behind his home in Australia. There he received the Holy Spirit and began to speak in tongues.

Believe it or not, you can get so desperate to be filled with the Spirit that it doesn't matter what people say or how loud they get. You can receive when you are hungry for the Spirit.

Other hindrances. Besides the above objections that people sometimes give for not being able to receive, other hindrances may prevent them from receiving. One may be the denominational instruction that a person has been taught against speaking in tongues. But this is not a problem as real as it may seem. The subconscious prejudices often evaporate when a person's spiritual hunger reaches the level that the individual truly desires the power of the Holy Spirit more than anything else.

Another hindrance may be the opinion of family members or close friends. Without trying to sound uncharitable, remember that your primary objective is to obey God. He will help you with family members and/or associates who do not understand your interest in the Baptism in the Holy Spirit. The positive side of the Holy Spirit Baptism in your life is that the change in you often leads to others in your family becoming hungry for this new anointing. Let the Lord take care of your family members. Your obligation is to please Him.

Chapter Four

Steps to Being Filled With the Spirit

Now you are ready for your own Pentecost. As seen in the previous chapter, it is really not hard to receive the Baptism in the Holy Spirit. The Lord never intended this experience to be relegated to a privileged few. Thus, He did not intend for it to be difficult. He did, however, expect believers to seek Him with all of their hearts.

The following are some suggestions of what it may take to be filled with the Spirit. These "steps," or recommendations, are not in any hierarchal order nor are they intended to be procedures which the candidate implements mechanically. But, hopefully, they will be valuable in helping one concentrate to do everything in his/her power to cooperate with the baptizer, the Lord Jesus.

1. Create an atmosphere of praise by worshiping and adoring Jesus. The disciples did this prior to Pentecost. "And they returned to Jerusalem with great joy and spent all their time in the temple *praising* God" (Lk. 24:52, NEB–emphasis mine). This exercise of glorifying God is very important if one is going to receive the Holy Spirit Baptism. It may seem unnatural at first but continue to praise Christ until it does not seem strange to your own ears.

Also, learn to speak praises in an audible voice and not just in your mind. Speaking in tongues was audible on the day of Pentecost: " . . . everyone *heard* them speak in his own language" (Acts 2:6). It is audible today, though the volume may not always be at the highest or extreme levels. It would stand to reason that the transition from audible praise in English to audible praise in another language might be easier. (This does not mean that the Holy Spirit cannot work if one does not praise the Lord aloud. It simply is a suggestion to help you, the candidate, have liberty in praising God.)

2. Expect to speak in tongues. Realize that the Holy Spirit eagerly waits to come sweeping over you, and Jesus is anxious to baptize you (Luke 11:13). Don't doubt for one moment that you will speak in another language. Expect it.

3. Leave your English or your native language altogether. When the Spirit comes over you,

you will need to determine that you are not going to try to stay with your native tongue regardless of how difficult it may be to speak in that language. It often has been pointed out that no one can speak two languages at once. Do not be afraid to leave the known to receive the unknown. Praise God from your innermost being with your lips prepared to speak when the words come.

4. Receive the Holy Spirit Baptism. This is your part. Don't wait for God to give the Holy Spirit to you. He has already given the Spirit. The Spirit was given on the day of Pentecost in baptismal power. It is up to you to receive. When someone gives you a gift, you don't have to beg for it in order to receive it. All you must do is reach out and take what is being offered. The same is true with the Holy Spirit Baptism. Don't beg, don't plead. Just thank God for His gift.

It was my privilege to be part of an all night service in a church that we started in a foreign country many years ago. The church, a megachurch of several thousand now, invited me to speak at 2:30 in the morning. I had already spoken in another church planting situation that previous evening but I was more than ready for the opportunity to speak and encourage people to receive the Baptism in the Spirit. About fifteen received that night, including a lady who was so desperate that she prayed loudly, begging God to fill her with the Spirit. I went over to her and softly spoke to her declaring, "You don't have to beg. God wants to fill you with the Spirit. Just worship Him." She began to worship the Lord. When I laid my hands on her, she immediately began to speak in tongues.

When we beg God for the gift He is already trying to give us, it almost seems that we doubt His generosity. Or, it implies that we don't really believe that He wants to fill us. The fact is, God delights in us and desires to give us the best gift, the Holy Spirit Baptism (Mt. 7:11, Lk. 11:13). Receive what He has for you!

5. If you hear strange utterances coming to your mind, speak them. Don't wait for the Holy Spirit to speak them for you. *The Holy Spirit will not speak for you.*

On the day of Pentecost when the 120 were filled, they began to speak with other tongues as the Spirit gave them utterance. "And they were all filled with the Holy Ghost and began to speak with other tongues as the Spirit gave them utterance" (Acts 2:4,

KJV). "They" is the subject both of "were . . . filled" and "began." So *they* were filled and *they* spoke. The Amplified Bible states that the Spirit kept giving them *appropriate words*. The Holy Spirit gave the words and they did the speaking.

Twenty years later, the pattern was still the same when the Ephesians received the infilling of the Spirit. "And when Paul had laid hands on them, the Holy Spirit came upon them, and *they spoke with tongues* and prophesied" (Acts 19:6, NKJV–emphasis mine).

You will never speak if you keep waiting for the Spirit to put you into some kind of trance and do it all for you. It will be your mouth, your tongue, your voice, but *His* words.

The miracle is not in the speaking but in the words that are spoken. When I attended language school to learn Spanish, we were required to learn the different mechanical positions of the mouth and tongue for pronouncing each letter in the Spanish alphabet. For example, the tongue must be placed in five different positions in the mouth in order to pronounce the letter "n" in Spanish, depending on the letter before or after. Though I learned the Spanish language to the best of my ability, sooner or later pronunciation or grammatical errors will identify me as someone who has learned the language but is not a native speaker.

But there have been many cases of people who have received the Baptism in the Holy Spirit and have spoken fluently in another language without a trace of an accent. A missionary friend of mine, Ralph Hiatt, was privileged to hear a young Argentine girl speak in perfectly fluent English when she received the Baptism in the Holy Spirit. There was no trace of an accent. When he questioned her after the service, she confirmed that she had never even heard English spoken before. The miracle was in the words she spoke without an accent.

For fourteen years I taught at a Pentecostal University and directed the Missions activities of that institution. Once I invited a minister from India, Dr. Jawahar Samuel, to speak. A lady on staff, Dr. Sheba Kulothungan, was from the same city, Coimbatur, India, where Dr. Samuel pastors. Since she was more fluent in English than Dr. Samuel, she served as his interpreter. After his message, Dr. Samuel ministered to the students praying for them personally. He had me to pray for him and I then asked that he pray for me. When he finished praying for me, I began to speak in tongues. Dr. Samuel became greatly excited when I was speaking in tongues. After a few minutes, I stopped speaking in tongues and Dr. Samuel and Dr. Kulothungan both told me that I was praising God in their native language of Tamil. I spoke clearly without an accent. This experience, called *Xenolalia* (speaking in a known language that the speaker does not understand but someone present does), often occurs. But whether anyone understands the believer who is baptized in the Spirit or not, the tongues speaker speaks in an actual language. The miracle is in the fact that the person speaking can form words fluently and enunciate them perfectly without a hint of an accent.

When one comes close to being filled with the Spirit, strange words of another language often come to his/her mind. A young man in one of my revivals spoke in tongues after I instructed him to say the words that the Lord may have given him in his mind. He said that he had first heard those words in his mind when he was just a boy in youth camp seeking to be filled with the Spirit. He had been afraid to speak them out loud. He was gloriously filled when he turned loose of his fears.

6. If your lips and your tongue start stam-

mering, the Holy Spirit is trying to get you to speak. You may not hear the words in your mind, but when you determine to yield to the Holy Spirit, at that moment the Holy Spirit will quicken you. Any time the Holy Spirit causes your lips to quiver and your tongue to stammer, He is trying to get you to speak and you can be assured that the words are present. They may not be in your mind but they will be in your mouth.

That is when faith must take hold. Tell the Lord that, by faith, you are going to speak - not in English (or your native tongue), but in another language as He gives the words. This is an absolute step of faith but the Lord will honor the faith that you exercise. Now, I am not by any means suggesting that you invent the words. But I am proposing that your willingness to speak and your determination to take a huge step of faith will often be rewarded with strange words coming out of your mouth. Remember, this act of faith to speak is linked to those occasions when you have stammering lips. Your lips may be quivering and moving rapidly. Your tongue may be thick and heavy and you may have difficulty even praising God in your native tongue. The Holy Spirit moves powerfully upon you at those moments, but He will not speak for you. He tries to prompt you to speak. Usually fear prevents one from completely yielding and speaking when stammering lips are present. A beautiful feeling of release occurs when the candidate takes the step of faith to speak and begins uttering words which he/she has never learned.

On one occasion I was addressing this very point in a teaching session with believers from various churches when a lady held up her hand. I recognized her and she said that she consistently had stammering lips but she could not get past that point. By faith I told her, "You will be filled today." I felt that the teaching on the subject and the power of the Holy Spirit would release her. When we later invited those who were hungry to be filled with the Spirit to come forward, the lady came to the front. After some time, she began to speak in tongues. She had to reach the point that she recognized the Spirit of God was upon her and that He was trying to get her to speak. No longer was she just stammering, she was speaking a language.

7. Speak, if only a few syllables are present at first. Don't be concerned if only a few syllables or words come at the beginning. The complete fluency will come.

Doyle Jones

Take note that initially the candidate who receives will generally be speaking praises to God in another language. In Acts 10:46, the Revised Standard Version says of Cornelius' household when they received the infilling that they were "extolling God." The same setting in the Phillips' translation states that they were "glorifying God."

"Hallelujah," "Praise the Lord," "Thank you Jesus," "Glory to God," and variations of these praise phrases show the limitations of the English language in praising God. In many other languages the same limits exist. In a new language the words may seem a bit redundant and repetitious at first. You probably are *praising* God in the new language at first. Eventually more fluency will come as the Spirit gives you a complete vocabulary and even prays through you for needs you know nothing about (Rom. 8:26, Jude 20).

Do not go back to English or your native language when you first begin speaking in tongues, whether there are many words or just a few. Continue to cooperate with the Spirit by using your mouth to form the words. Don't be afraid to move your tongue and lips. You can't speak in any language without using all of your organs of speech.

8. Speak, even if it doesn't sound like a language to you. There are many languages and dialects that may not sound like languages to you but that is only because you do not understand them. Being filled with the Spirit is not based on your ability to understand the language. It is based on speaking in obedience to the Spirit's promptings.

9. Realize that you control the flow of the Spirit through you. You are the one who allows the language to begin and you are the one who stops the words from being uttered. The more you choose to speak in tongues, the easier it becomes to yield to the Holy Spirit. Initially, you are using a praise language, but the language may change to other languages as the Spirit directs.

Very often, when a candidate speaks in tongues for the first time, initially he/she may stop after a few words have been spoken. This happens sometimes because of fear or perhaps because the individual feels that there is nothing to be gained by continuing. But the newly baptized believer should not back away from the experience; on the contrary, he/she needs to continue yielding to God. That decision to maintain the flow of the Spirit and to speak in tongues is placed in the hands of the individual. God does not force someone to persist in seeking Him.

10. Continue to pray in the Spirit every day. This is a necessary part of your spiritual development. Praying in the Spirit edifies (builds up) an individual (1 Cor. 14:4). One individual told me that it was self-ish to pray in tongues because it edified the person speaking. She did not understand that the word "edi-fies" means "build up" or "improve" (TAB).

Let me emphasize that receiving the Baptism in the Holy Spirit is a spiritual experience. The candidate must be absolutely sincere when seeking the Baptism in the Holy Spirit. He/she cannot receive just on the basis of mechanically employing the ten recommendations cited above. It is beneficial to famil-iarize oneself with these suggestions before seeking. But, by all means, one must not concentrate so hard on the mechanics that Jesus is not worshipped with the whole heart. You must totally yield to Him. The suggestions may come to your mind or you may not even have time to even think of these things when the Holy Spirit comes over you.

Receiving the Holy Spirit does not have to be a prolonged experience and many times it is not. At other times you may have difficulty concentrating on the Lord. If you find yourself up against a "brick wall," call to mind some of the items mentioned above. Perhaps they will be of benefit. The most important thing, however, is continuous praise and worship of Jesus, the Baptizer.

Chapter Five

Be Being Filled With the Spirit

Be Being Filled

Ephesians 5:18 says in the KJV, "Be filled with the Spirit." But this has been variously translated as, "Be getting filled with the Spirit" (*The Emphasized New Testament*), and "Ever be filled with the Spirit" (Williams Translation). The *Amplified Bible* renders this, "Ever be filled and stimulated with the (Holy) Spirit."

The Greek verb here (*pleroo*) is redundant and the feeling of this Scripture is "be *being* filled." The Wycliffe Bible Commentary translates Ephesians 5:18, "Keep on being filled; be continuously filled with the Spirit."

The flow of the Spirit should be constant. This means that we need to practice yielding to the Spirit every day. Too many believers have received the Spirit with the evidence of speaking in tongues but have failed to continue the practice. Some never again speak in tongues after their initial experience. This should not occur. The Spirit-baptized believer should obey the injunction to "be being filled." The same effort and desire that produced the first infilling should be expended on a daily basis to assure that the experience occurs repeatedly. As one constantly exercises faith to yield to the Holy Spirit, it becomes easier to speak in the new language that God has given.

Being Filled and Doubt

After the infilling of the Spirit, the devil uses doubt against the tongue-speaking believer as his chief tool. Questions arise in the mind of the believer. "Am I really filled?" "Did I just imagine those words?" "Was I just imitating someone around me?" These kinds of questions should be anticipated by the believer. Many times Satan has used the same type of insinuations to make Christians doubt their salvation or other promises that God has given.

After one receives the Baptism in the Holy Spirit, Satan knows he failed in his effort to prevent the infilling of the Spirit. However, he does not give up. He immediately works on keeping the believer's new-found power in check. His most effective weapon to accomplish this is doubt. So uncertainty begins to plague the recently filled believer's mind concerning his/her recent experience.

Even when the candidate is certain that he/she has received, the devil persists with another kind of doubt. He will say, "Is that all there is to it? I thought you were supposed to receive power. Why, you are no different than before!"

One lady who received the Holy Spirit Baptism in one of my revivals came to me and said, "Something needs to be written for people to help them *after* they have received." Knowing the devil had been putting doubts in her mind since the few days before when I had helped her receive the infilling of the Spirit, I quickly began to give her instructions. I told her that many times a person will not feel the tremendous emotional uplift the day after receiving the Baptism in the Holy Spirit. But power will be there nonetheless. I referred to Acts 1:8 (KJV) which declares, "Ye shall receive power *after* that the Holy Ghost is come upon you." Then I described how that power would be present in some individuals in unnoticeable, subtle ways - power over temptations, power over an uncontrollable temper, etc. Immediately her face lit up. She described a situation she had faced which, before her infilling, would have caused her to be irritable and to react angrily. But instead she found herself very calm, without any volatile reaction at all. She realized then, through our conversation, that the Holy Spirit was certainly at work.

When confronted by doubts, what can be done? Here are some suggestions:

1. DOUBT YOUR DOUBTS! Realize the source of your doubts. Remember you were praising and worshipping God when you received. The doubts do not come from Him. If you just have to doubt, then doubt your doubts.

2. DISMISS YOUR DOUBTS! Don't entertain your doubts. Don't even think of them. Think on the things of God (Phil. 4:8).

3. DEFEAT YOUR DOUBTS! Start praising God immediately. Let His Spirit flood your soul. It may take a few minutes to "prime the pump," but don't become discouraged. Keep praising God until you begin to speak with other tongues once more.

Being Filled and Being Lackadaisical

If Satan cannot prevent you from doubting your experience, he will do his best to keep you from using your new-found power. First, he may try to make you feel ashamed of having spoken in tongues as if that makes you less intelligent or inferior in some way. What a lie! One should never be ashamed of the miracle of speaking in tongues. Remember, all the apostles spoke in tongues. The writers of the New Testament had the experience. The person who speaks in tongues is in excellent company.

When you receive, you should have more boldness to witness (Acts 1:8), but some folks will never comprehend this new ability because Satan talks them out of it before they ever get started. He knows the tools are there, he just doesn't want the newly-filled believer to know how to use them.

Even when you try to witness, you may be disappointed that you are not more effective. But use of the power of the Holy Spirit in witnessing is like a muscle: the more you allow the Holy Spirit to use you, the stronger you become.

You may not recognize any outward change in the effectiveness of your witnessing, but if you will stay full of the Holy Spirit, the words that you say will work on a person's spirit long after you have talked to them. The power may be in the *eventual impact* of the words, rather than their immediate delivery. As the writer of Hebrews declares, "For the Word that God speaks is alive and full of power (making it active, operative, energizing, and effective) . . ." (Heb. 4:12, TAB). The Holy Spirit will teach you how to use your God-given authority over the power of the enemy (John 14:26).

Another danger facing the newly baptized believer involves satanic efforts to cause the Spirit-filled believer to believe that he/she has "arrived," with no further need to keep growing in God. The temptation to believe that one has finally reached the ultimate attainment in the Holy Spirit may develop.

In Pentecostal circles the first encounter of speaking in tongues is often referred to as the initial, physical evidence of the infilling in the Holy Spirit. The "initial evidence" means that what you received, your Baptism in the Spirit, only signified the beginning. The "physical" evidence means that the tongues part was just the physical manifestation that you have received the Holy Spirit Baptism.

The more you yield to God and let His Spirit

flow through you, the more many other evidences and spiritual dynamics are actualized in your life. For example, the infilling with the Spirit enhances one's love for Christ and one's desire to please Him. Also, the fruit of the Spirit (Gal. 5:22–23), or spiritual character qualities, can be developed more rapidly.

Being Filled and Trials

Sometimes great trials follow one's infilling with the Holy Spirit. Satan makes an all out effort to stop the newly-filled believer. Notice the following biblical examples: Jesus was led into the wilderness after the Spirit descended upon Him (Matthew 4). The apostles left the upper room to run into opposition by the Jewish leaders. After Paul received his Baptism in the Spirit, believers mistrusted him (Acts 9:26) and the Grecian Jews tried to kill him (Acts 9:29).

You, as a newly baptized believer, may have opposition and/or tests from various sources. Satan may work overtime to impugn your reputation, take away your employment, or cause friction between you and your parents, your children, your spouse or other family members. James encouraged believers to " . . . count it all joy when you fall into various trials" (James 1:2, NKJV). The Holy Spirit gives power to obey that Scripture. Regardless of how difficult the trial may be, you will have power to face it. As John wrote, " . . . He who is in you is greater than he who is in the world" (1 John 4:4, NKJV).

Chapter Six

"Be Filled With the Spirit" -
Option or Command?

Teaching by Contrasts

When Paul wrote the words, "Be filled with the Spirit" (Eph. 5:18, KJV), he was contrasting extreme lifestyles. He deals with hideous sins that should "not even be named among . . . saints" (Eph. 5:3, NKJV). Paul reminds the Ephesians of their past ways, using the difference between light and darkness to describe the changes Christ has made. He admonishes them to live "not as unwise but as wise" (verse 15, NIV). In a well-known Hebrew writing style found frequently in Psalms, Proverbs, and other passages, Paul contrasts negative choices, lifestyles, etc., with their positive opposites.[6] Just as being drunk falls on the far end of the negative spectrum, being filled with the Spirit appears high on the other end of the positive scale. The Spirit-filled Christian should not dwell in darkness and defeat but in praise and victory: "Speaking to one another in psalms and hymns and spiritual songs, singing and making melody in your heart to the Lord, giving thanks always for all things to God the Father in the name of our Lord Jesus Christ" (Eph. 5:19–20, NKJV). A great difference exists between the walk of the Spirit-filled Christian and the life of an unclean sinner filled with an evil spirit or fleshly desires.

Paul, by the contrasts he made in these verses in chapter five, fully expected an absolute rejection of the carnal lifestyle. He did not intend a moderate approach to serving God. The Spirit-filled life is the answer to a boring, lifeless, pathetic nominal Christianity.

A Profound Ingestion, The Only Option

When Paul said, "Be *filled* with the Spirit," he was advocating more than just a casual approach to being filled with the Spirit. The Greek indicates redundancy, a continual process of being filled with the Spirit.[7] The procedure was to be repetitive. The Weymouth Bible renders it, "Drink deeply of the Spirit," indicating a long, lingering drink. This injunction of Paul points to a profound ingestion of the Holy Spirit, not just a taste.

Paul makes it clear in his epistles that the only option for the believer is to practice the Spirit-filled life and not the carnal, lust-filled life. Notice his advice to the Galatians:

> So I say, live by the Spirit, and you will not gratify the desires of the sinful nature. For the sinful nature desires what is contrary to the Spirit, and the Spirit what is contrary to the sinful nature. They are in conflict with each other, so that you do not do what you want (Gal. 5:16–17, NIV).
>
> The one who sows to please his sinful nature, from that nature will reap destruction, the one who sows to please the Spirit, from the Spirit will reap eternal life (Gal. 6:8, NIV).

Paul clearly admonishes his audience to seek the Spirit-filled life in these verses. Without a determination to be constantly filled with the Spirit, the believer can be tempted to sow to his flesh, for the flesh "fights against the Spirit" (*Conybeare's Translation*). Paul knew the danger of an indifferent, apathetic attitude toward being filled with the Spirit.

God did not intend for us to treat something so wonderful and so powerful as the Baptism in the Holy Spirit as if it were an experience we could accept or reject nonchalantly according to our own feelings. Paul does not leave an option in the matter. When he said, "Be filled with the Spirit," the context, as well as the command form of the Greek verb, does not leave room for choice. These words, written by the venerable apostle from his prison cell, would have been taken seriously by the Ephesian believers.

Comparing Believers

Many times I have heard people make comparisons between certain individuals who have been baptized in the Spirit and others who are not. Some have remarked that certain individuals who do not speak in tongues do as much or more for God than many individuals who do speak in tongues. On the basis of this argument, some honestly contend that they do not need to speak with tongues.

In response, first note that if God had not intended for everyone to be filled and speak in tongues, surely He would have made exceptions among the 120 in the upper room. With the diversity of personalities represented, one would assume some would have needed the experience but others did not. But, without exception, everyone in the upper room (Acts 2) spoke with other tongues. Ardent Peter was filled as well as tranquil John. Thomas, sometimes called "doubting" Thomas (perhaps unfairly), received the Holy Spirit Baptism as did Mary, the mother of Jesus. Similar arguments could be presented based on the infilling of the Gentiles in Acts 10 and the experience of the Ephesians in Acts 19. They all received.

Second, an individual's potential should not be confused with the Holy Spirit's power. The individual who does so much for God without the infilling of the Spirit would doubtless do much more if he were baptized in the Spirit. The Spirit-filled individual who does not accomplish much for God may not have the capacity or potential to achieve as much for God as someone else. The Holy Spirit will use any Christian among us regardless of temperament or character but He does not wind us up and make robots of us. Some will accomplish more for God than others. But, without doubt, individuals filled with the Spirit will do more for God after their own infilling than that which he/she accomplished before being baptized in the Spirit. If this does not happen, then the Holy Spirit is not being allowed to move in the individual properly.[8]

God's Plan Versus Ours

The real objection to being filled with the Spirit for some is speaking in tongues. Very few Christians would object to being filled with the Spirit if they did not have to speak in tongues. But if we receive the Spirit, it must be on God's terms, not our own. He is the One who established the standard. He is the One who speaks through His eternal Word to this and every generation declaring, "Be filled with the Spirit."

Being filled with the Spirit, with the accompanying evidence of speaking in tongues is God's plan. Not only is it His plan, it is His command. Jesus told the disciples, "Tarry in the city of Jerusalem until you are endued with power from on high" (Lk. 24:49, NKJV). If the disciples who had sat at the feet of the Master for 3 1/2 years needed to be filled with the Spirit, how much more do we need to be filled? Jesus did not give the disciples an option. He did not say, "Tarry, if you think you need to." He expected obedience of them just as he expects obedience of us.

If we felt that being filled with the Spirit were an option, the tendency would be to lose interest if we failed to receive the experience immediately. But if we realize that this experience is commanded in God's Word, then we should never be satisfied until we have complied with God's desire for us.

Being Filled: Prerequisite for Heaven?

This discussion naturally leads to the question, "Can a person go to heaven without being baptized in the Holy Spirit?" Some Pentecostals teach that one must speak in tongues in order to be saved.[9] But this does not correlate with the Scriptures (Rom. 10:9, 10; 1 John 1:9; John 1:12). The Baptism in the Holy Spirit is subsequent to the conversion experience as discussed earlier. A born again believer can enter heaven based on his/her confession of faith in the crucified and resurrected Christ as Savior and Lord.

The question should not be, "Can a person go to heaven without the Baptism in the Holy Spirit?" but "Why would any Christian want to be without the Holy Spirit?" My home pastor, Rev. Allen Sanders (now deceased), used to say, "I wouldn't want to go across the street without the Baptism in the Holy

Spirit." Another question one should ask is, "In a world geared to sensuality, sin and satanic assault, can I make it without the Baptism in the Holy Spirit?" Getting to heaven is not the ultimate goal of the born again believer. If that depicts our reason for serving Christ, then we have not fully comprehended the reason we are Christians. Our supreme goal should be to please our Master and exemplify His life within us. The empowerment of the Holy Spirit helps that realization to materialize.

Jesus said of the Holy Spirit, "But when the Helper comes, whom I shall send to you from the Father, the Spirit of truth who proceeds from the Father, He will testify of Me" (John 15:26, (NKJV). Also, He declared, "When He, the Spirit of truth has come, He will guide you into all truth . . . He will glorify me" (John 16:13–14, NKJV). The Holy Spirit points the hungry believer towards Jesus Christ. The more we allow Him, the Holy Spirit, to be in control of our lives, the more He will point us towards Christ. We must have all the power the Holy Spirit has for us if we are going to fully glorify Christ in this life. That power comes through the Baptism in the Holy Spirit: "But you shall receive power when the Holy Spirit has come upon you . . ." (Acts 1:8, NKJV).

Chapter Seven

How to Help People to Be Filled With the Spirit

The desire to share the Pentecostal experience with other believers naturally follows one's own Baptism in the Holy Spirit. Sharing the experience when the encounter is fresh and new should be expected. Unfortunately, some who have been filled with the Holy Spirit for years sometimes take the experience for granted and do not stress to others the necessity of being filled with the Spirit. All Spirit-baptized believers should readily encourage other believers to seek the infilling in the Holy Spirit.

Some Spirit-filled believers do well at inspiring others to seek the Baptism in the Holy Spirit but do not have much success in actually helping people receive. I have heard some say, "Well, that's not my ministry." In reality, though, anyone baptized in the Holy Spirit can help others receive the Holy Spirit. The following are some observations pertinent to those who want to help potential candidates receive

the Baptism in the Holy Spirit. The first six suggestions concern attitudes that often hinder the Spirit-
filled believer from helping others. The other recommendations concern positive steps to take in helping
others receive the Holy Spirit Baptism.

Possess Correct Attitudes

First, *hold the Holy Spirit in proper respect.*
He is a Person, not an "it," nor an "entity." Webster's
dictionary says that a person is (1) "a living human
being," or (2) "the composite of characteristics that
make up an individual personality." But he also
refers to person as "the separate individualities of the
Father, Son, and Holy Spirit, as distinguished from
the essence of the Godhead that unites them." Even
Webster recognizes the Holy Spirit as a Person.

Many Scriptures point to qualities of the Holy
Spirit that reveal that He is a Person.

The Holy Spirit possesses knowledge.

But God has revealed them to us through
His Spirit. For the Spirit searches all things,
yes, the deep things of God. For what man
knows the things of a man, except the spirit

of the man which is in him? Even so no one knows the things of God except the Spirit of God (1 Cor. 2:10, 11, NKJV).

The Holy Spirit possesses a will.

"But one and the same Spirit works all these things, distributing to each one individually as He wills" (1 Cor. 12:11, NKJV). This Scripture shows us that the Holy Spirit is not like gravity or electricity or some force that we can use as we will. Rather He is a person who uses us as He wills.

The Holy Spirit possesses a mind.

"Now He who searches the hearts knows what the mind of the Spirit is, because He makes intercession for the saints according to the will of God" (Rom. 8:27, NKJV). The Greek word for mind here, *phronema* (fron'ay mah), includes the idea of thought, purpose and feeling.

The Holy Spirit possesses feeling.

"And grieve not the Holy Spirit of God, whereby ye are sealed unto the day of redemption" (Eph. 4:30, KJV).

The Holy Spirit can act.

Notice some of the list of activities of the Spirit: (1) 1 Cor. 2:10—The Spirit searches all things. (2) Acts 2:4, Rev. 2:7—The Holy Spirit speaks. (3) Gal. 4:6—The Holy Spirit witnesses. (4) Rom. 8:26—The Holy Spirit intercedes. (5) John 15:26—The Holy Spirit testifies. (6) Rom. 8:14—The Holy Spirit guides. (7) Acts 16:6, 7; Acts 13:2—The Holy Spirit commands. (8) Acts 20:28—The Holy Spirit appoints. (9) 2 Peter 1:21—The Holy Spirit reveals. (10) John 14:26—The Holy Spirit teaches. (11) Acts 9:31—The Holy Spirit comforts.

Notice also that one can react to the Holy Spirit. (1) The Holy Spirit can be grieved (Eph. 4:30). (2) One can rebel against the Holy Spirit (Isa. 63:10). (3) The Holy Spirit can be profaned, insulted, and outraged (Heb. 10:29, TAB). (4) One can lie to the Holy Spirit (Acts 5:3). (5) The Holy Spirit can be blasphemed (Mt. 12:31, 32). (6) The Holy Spirit can be quenched (1 Thess. 5:19). (7) One can receive the Holy Spirit (Acts 2:38; 8:15).

These and many other verses should remind us that we must always treat the Holy Spirit with respect. He is worthy of our highest regard. This attitude must prevail if we are going to help others.

In our own walk with the Lord, we need to remind ourselves that the Holy Spirit is not a dove, He is not fire, He is not wind, He is not a sound, and He is not tongues. All these things may symbolize His presence, but He is a person! Our goal is to be open to the Holy Spirit as a person Who is directing and leading our lives.

A second important factor for helping hungry candidates is to *be filled with the Spirit yourself and make sure you have an up-to-date experience*. As a general rule, you can only lead people as far as you yourself have gone. God may make an exception and touch someone in spite of you but the desired goal is that He use us constantly. Therefore, we need to "be being filled" with the Spirit.

A third factor is to *be convinced that God wants everyone to be filled with the Spirit*. This has been dealt with previously but some individuals, even after their own Spirit-Baptism may still feel that it is really not important for all believers to have the infilling of the Spirit. (See Acts 2:39.) You must never entertain the thought that someone with whom you are praying just might be an exception. You might say, "Perhaps God does not want them to be filled." If you entertain such a thought, you will not be as determined to help them receive.

One time I preached a youth camp in which about fifty young people received the infilling in the Holy Spirit. After one of the services, I prayed with one young man for two hours to receive the promise of the Father. I encouraged him with words like, "Come on, Jim. The Holy Spirit is here. Listen to Him. Perhaps the Holy Spirit is giving you words, even now. If so, speak them out. God is with you, Jim." After about two hours, the young man received a glorious infilling. Finally, after the euphoria had lifted somewhat, the young man told me, "By the way, my name's not Jim!" Perhaps I was the problem! Maybe I distracted him! However, I can say that the one thing that kept me praying for that young man so long is the same thing that spurs my determination today: I am convinced that God wants everyone filled with the Spirit!

Let me hasten to explain here that the length of time spent by the candidate to receive does not mean God is not ready to fill him/her. The candidate often has problems yielding or crossing the fear boundary. We should be there encouraging and helping everyone who struggles, convinced that God responds to hungry hearts.

A fourth factor is to *be convinced that being filled with the Holy Spirit is subsequent to salvation*. This also has been addressed but it needs to be re-emphasized in this context. You will not be as effective in helping others to receive this experience without an absolute conviction that the Holy Spirit in baptism power does not come at conversion.

A fifth factor is to *be convinced that the evidence of being filled with the Spirit is speaking in tongues*. When gripped by this certainty, you will desire for all to speak in tongues. This is a glorious experience and we should never be ashamed of having the same experience as Peter, the apostles, the Apostle Paul and the early church. And we should be quick to tell new converts or the doubtful about the value and validity of speaking in tongues.

A sixth factor for helping others to receive the Baptism in the Holy Spirit is to *be convinced of the necessity of being filled with the Spirit*. Is it really important that a person be filled with the Spirit? Your only answer should be a resounding, "Yes!"

Recognize that Christ did not want the disciples preaching, witnessing, or disciplining anyone until they had been "endued (clothed) with power from on high" (Luke 24:49, KJV, see also, NIV).

This does not mean that God forbids any activity by believers before they are filled with the Spirit. It just emphasizes the value Christ placed on the infilling of the Holy Spirit.

The importance of the Baptism in the Holy Spirit has not diminished for Saints today. The Holy Spirit in baptismal power will help a carnal Christian become a better person. The dynamic power of the Holy Spirit can change a carnal, worldly church and reinstate holy living, joyful worship, and missionary vision to its adherents.

Preparing Candidates to Receive

The most important ingredient for helping individuals receive is to *pray earnestly that hungry candidates will receive the Baptism in the Holy Spirit*. Pray especially for those who have sought the infilling of the Spirit for many years but have failed to receive. Great moves of the Holy Spirit occur in response to prayer.

Next, always *give proper instruction prior to praying with candidates who are seeking the infilling of the Holy Spirit*. Use the material found in this book. Mention those things that hinder an individual from receiving. Also, reiterate the recommendations alluded to in chapter five.

Another ingredient is to *expect people to be filled*. Have faith that the Lord will pour out his Spirit. We must not allow our faith to be diminished when believing for candidates to receive the Holy Spirit. We must never despair that a potential candidate will receive.

The thought may occur to you, "Maybe this person is not going to receive for reasons unknown to me." Sometimes people seek the Spirit and fail to receive. Perhaps some of the hindrances mentioned already prevent them from receiving. If we sense that they are not making progress, it might help to talk with them and tell them some of the things that Satan uses against us when we seek the Holy Spirit. Afterwards, begin once again to pray with the individual.

Another important element in preparing people to receive the infilling of the Spirit is to *preach/teach about the Baptism in the Holy Spirit*. Many pastors or individuals in leadership positions in churches yearn to see their constituents filled with the Holy Spirit. However, they seldom preach or teach on the Baptism in the Holy Spirit. Or, if they do minister on the subject, they fail to give any instruction concerning what to expect. Their sermons or lectures may only extol the importance of being filled or the euphoria that accompanies the experience. They may even give confusing information such as, "Allow the Holy Spirit to speak through you." This sort of advice puts in the mind of the believer the thought that they will have some kind of "out of the body" experience with no control whatsoever on their own availability and/or ability to yield. The pastor or instructor must give clear signals when sharing a message about the Baptism in the Holy Spirit.

The minister or teacher who wants to see people filled with the Spirit must make his presentation interesting, exciting and informational. The presenter who does not sound convinced that the Baptism in the Holy Spirit is a tremendous help and experience in his own life may find it difficult to persuade others to receive.

Finally, those who assist others to receive the infilling of the Holy Spirit should not hesitate to **lay hands on the individual seeker**. The practice of laying on of hands in the Old Testament often signified a commissioning or transferring of power. This is seen when Moses laid hands on Joshua in preparation for Joshua's future leadership (Num. 27:22). After the death of Moses, the seal of Joshua's leadership referred back to Moses' act of laying his hands on Joshua. "Now Joshua son of Nun was filled with the spirit of wisdom because Moses had laid his hands on him. So the Israelites listened to him and did what the Lord had commanded Moses" (Deut. 34:9). New power and authority were recognizable after the imposition of hands.

The same authoritative provision is associated with the infilling of the Spirit in the New Testament. Jesus promised power for those who received the Holy Spirit (Acts 1:8). Reception of this power often coincided with the imposition of hands. Paul laid hands on the Ephesian believers when they received the infilling of the Spirit (Acts 19:6). When Peter and the Apostles went down to Samaria, they laid hands on the new believers and they were filled with the Spirit (Acts 8:17). Also, Ananias laid his hands on Paul in order for Paul to receive his infilling (Acts 9:17).

There were instances in which people received the infilling without having hands laid upon them (Acts 2:4; Acts 10:44). Those occasions remind us that the Holy Spirit often moves on people without our direct participation. But the other aforementioned examples tell us that He encourages our involvement and responds at the moment that we lay hands on believers.

Other Observations

Not everyone you pray with will receive the Holy Spirit immediately. This should not discourage you. You cannot control an individual's personal response to the Lord, the baptizer. At the same time, you should never become nonchalant about those who do not receive. You should make a mental note to intercede for that individual in your private devotions. Also, be sure to instruct the individual to seek the Holy Spirit in private. Many people have received the Spirit in their home or even in their car. You must encourage those who do not receive to maintain their spiritual hunger and not get discouraged.

Another important item is to give proper instruction to those who want to assist others to receive. I have seen individuals on the threshold of receiving the Baptism in the Holy Spirit when a well-meaning believer would shout something to them that would be distracting. Sometimes their advice is totally unscriptural. If you are the pastor or instructor, this can be prevented by training your altar workers prior to the prayer time. I often ask Spirit-filled believers to stand behind the candidates, affirming them by praying in the Spirit themselves. I specifically request that they not try to give them instruction but to allow me to minister to them.

On occasion, I have workers to help me in a different manner. One time a group of students from the university where I formerly taught accompanied me to Mexico. In a few nights of ministry in three locations, nearly thirty received the Baptism in the Holy Spirit. Since the services were in Spanish, most of the students did not understand what was happening and would not have been able to communicate with those who came forward to receive the Holy Spirit Baptism. In one church, I had the students to stand in front of the candidates who had come forward and prepare to lay their hands on them after I prayed for them. I stood on the platform and prayed and, as I had instructed the students, they laid their hands on these hungry Mexican believers simultaneously when I gave them the signal. Nearly all of the individuals touched by these students began to speak in tongues.

The ingredients for this to happen were all in place. First, the students and I prayed earnestly, before and during the church service, for hungry believers to be filled. Second, we prayed for a special anointing to rest upon us as we prayed for others. Third, we exercised faith by giving God the opportunity to simultaneously fill these individuals. Fourth, the hunger of the candidates had been reinforced by preaching a faith-building message about receiving the Baptism in the Holy Spirit. Fifth, the candidates had been given instruction about receiving the Baptism in the Holy Spirit. Most importantly, our great God responded and miraculously swept over the congregation.

Chapter Eight

Why All Believers Should Be Filled with the Spirit and Speak in Tongues

Some Christians in Pentecostal churches become quite comfortable without the dynamic experience of speaking in tongues; i.e, being filled with the Spirit. They excuse themselves for a variety of reasons, some of which have been mentioned previously. They may think, "Why should I speak in tongues?" This question could be turned around -"Why not?" If indeed this experience is available to all believers, why would everyone not want to be filled? What advantages exist in receiving the *glossolalia* experience?

A number of reasons could be given explaining why a person should speak in tongues. Twelve of these are shared in the ensuing paragraphs. Some of these benefits may also apply to non-baptized believers with the exception that a more powerful flow of the Spirit in a Spirit-filled believer's life has the potential for more dramatic results.

With the above remarks in mind, note the following list which gives the rationale for speaking in tongues. Perhaps these observations will serve as an encouragement to those who have received as well as for those who are still candidates for the experience.

First, as noted previously in other chapters in this book, *speaking in tongues is scriptural*. This experience is not something conjured up by wild-eyed fanatics. It began on the day of Pentecost and continues until today. Those who speak with tongues reflect the same phenomena as those who received the experience in the book of Acts. One should speak in tongues knowing it is the scriptural pattern as seen in the book of Acts.

Next, *this experience is given by Jesus.* He promised the presence of the Holy Spirit, the Comforter, "whom I will send unto you from the Father" (John 15:26, NKJV). And in Acts 1:8, Jesus, the baptizer in the Holy Spirit, promised power when the Holy Spirit came on them. His promise was fulfilled on the day of Pentecost as He gave them the Holy Spirit. Speaking in tongues came with the package as Christ gave them the Holy Spirit power.

Another reason all believers should speak in tongues is that *it is commanded*. While Paul did not say, "Thou shalt speak in tongues," he did say, "Be filled with the Spirit." The whole point of this book is to show that being filled with the Holy Spirit in the context of Paul's or Luke's writings would involve speaking in tongues. Paul urged the Ephesians to be filled with the Spirit. Our Lord made the same demand on the disciples. He said, "Tarry in the city of Jerusalem until you are endued with power from on high" (Luke 24:49, NKJV).

Fourth, one should speak in tongues because *the experience is associated with spiritual power in one's life*. This was promised to the disciples prior to Pentecost (Acts 1:8) and is certainly evidenced in their lives afterwards as "many wonders and signs were done by the apostles" (Acts 2:43, NKJV). Paul made the Gospel known to the Gentiles "by the power of the Spirit of God . . ." (Rom. 15:19, NKJV). The same power seen in the lives of believers in the first century can be expected when one receives the Spirit today.

One should speak in tongues because *it intensifies the desire to carry out Christ's mandate to reach the world*. Christ declared that this would happen after the disciples received the Baptism in the Holy Spirit (Acts 1:8). The disciples went everywhere making converts and discipling them (Acts 2:42–47).

The same fervor accompanies the infilling of the Spirit today. The Pentecostal/Charismatics are currently the fastest growing segment of Christianity in the world. Peter Wagner, professor of church growth and the School of World Missions at Fuller Theological Seminary, by his own admission spent the first twenty years of his ministry as an anti-Pentecostal. However, Wagner was urged by Donald McGavran, father of the church growth movement, to study the Pentecostal churches in Latin America, many of which were having phenomenal growth. Wagner declared,

> The more I studied the Pentecostals, the more fascinated I became. My fascination soon turned to genuine appreciation, and appreciation led to a degree of participation. I have never quite become Pentecostal, but I certainly enjoy them and am blessed by being with them.
>
> My research has led me to make this bold statement: In all of human history, no other non-political, non militaristic, voluntary human movement has grown

as rapidly as the Pentecostal-charismatic movement in the last 25 years.[10]

Pentecostals have grown until some 625 million Pentecostals/Charismatics were tabulated worldwide in 2005.[11] Wagner and others who may not agree that speaking in tongues is the initial physical evidence of the infilling in the Holy Spirit have taken note that Pentecostal/Charismatics are having an incredible missionary impact. This is not accidental. It coincides with Christ's promise to the disciples that they would be witnesses after they had received the Spirit. Spirit-filled believers today should want that same experience in order to be better equipped to carry out Christ's mandate.

A sixth reason for the *glossolalia* experience is that *the Spirit-filled believer becomes a vehicle for the Holy Spirit's intercession.* The Apostle Paul said,

Likewise the Spirit also helps in our weaknesses. For we do not know what we should pray for as we ought, but the Spirit Himself makes intercession for us with groanings which cannot be uttered. Now He who searches the hearts knows what the mind of the Spirit is, because He makes intercession for the saints according to the will of God (Rom. 8:26–27, NKJV).

In these verses, Paul clearly states that there will be times when we do not know how to pray nor do we know who or what the object of our intercession is. Therefore the Spirit aids us in the time of our weakness (or "limitations" [Ph]), enabling us to pray with inexpressible "groanings" coming from the Spirit Himself. This intense intercession quite clearly occurs on behalf of the saints of God.

Without doubt this intercessory nature of the Holy Spirit often uses believers to pray the will of the Father for needs of others. When my wife, Cherie, and I were appointed missionaries, we learned of several instances in which the Spirit led people to intercede for us.

On one occasion Gary Jones, a former missionary, and I were taken out to be shot in a country besieged by war and revolution. Two young revolutionaries took us to an abandoned garbage dump to "put a bullet in our heads," as they put it. They robbed us but changed their minds about shooting us at the last instance. Why? Because the Holy Spirit directed a number of people to pray for us at the very moment when we were about to be shot. An entire congregation was prompted to pray for us at the moment that our captors planned to shoot us. Cherie, at home in another country where we were living, felt impressed to spend the night in prayer. Her father, Rev. Lonnie Fogger, a pastor in Louisiana at the time, felt a burden to pray for us at the moment of our danger. Some time close to this development, Zillah Williams, a lady in Houston, Texas, felt a need to pray for me. Without doubt the intercession of these Spirit-filled, Spirit-led individuals praying in tongues and with their own understanding made the difference in our deliverance.

The Spirit can readily use individuals whose spiritual antennas vibrate to the Spirit's guidance. The Spirit-filled person can learn to be closely attuned to the intercessory nature of the Holy Spirit.

Next, note that *the* glossolalia *experience helps develop the fruit of the Spirit in the believer's life.* The fruit of the Spirit, spoken of in Galatians 5:22–23, is not limited to those who speak in tongues. But the nine different graces or virtues seen in Galatians 5 (love, joy, peace, patience, goodness, kindness, faith [faithfulness], humility, and self-control), must be developed in the Christian's life. When the Holy Spirit comes upon us, an immediate benefit is divine power.[12] This power is not limited to service. It also enables us to actively build character in our lives. Though a non-Spirit-filled believer can and should demonstrate the fruit of the Spirit in his life, he needs the added power to develop and maintain these graces that the Baptism in the Holy Spirit affords. The Spirit-filled believer has the opportunity for greater power or anointing to develop the fruit of the Spirit in his/her life.

The infilling of the Spirit *helps the individual to properly evaluate what is most important.* In his teaching to the Roman Christians, Paul admonished these new believers to not be so determined to eat food called unclean by an offended brother. The food in itself might not have been a stumbling block to the Christian wanting to eat it. However, Paul said, " . . . if your brother is grieved because of your food, you are no longer walking in love" (Rom. 14:15, NKJV). After all, the food was not the important item as Paul explained. "For the kingdom of God is not eating and drinking, but righteousness, peace, and joy in the Holy Spirit" (Rom. 14:17, NKJV). Righteousness, peace, and joy in the Holy Spirit far outweigh any satisfaction gained by material indulgences. A genuine experience in the Holy Spirit will help the Christian relate to these values.

I have experienced numerous occasions in which my set of values have been out of focus. When I spent time seeking God, praying in another language, the problem disappeared as an issue. The powerful Spirit filled me with such ecstasy that I wondered afterwards how such a wrong desire or attitude could have been so appealing to me. When one truly experiences the "joy in the Holy Spirit," mundane gratifications lose their attractiveness.

Now, notice that *praying in tongues can bring comfort in the time of trial*. Four times in the book of John, the Greek word *parakletos* (transliterated) is used to describe the Holy Spirit (Jn. 14:16, 26; Jn. 15:26; Jn. 16:7). The only other use of the word describes Christ in 1 John 2:1. Only the KJV translates *parakletos,* "comforter" while other translations usually prefer to use "counselor," "advocate," or "lawyer." But some translations also use the word "helper" and the idea is "one who strengthens." The word is so multifaceted that Robert Cook admits, " . . . no one translation does justice to its rich meaning."[13] Quite possibly the closest meaning conveyed is "a very interested helper who represents us in the time of trial."

The early church enjoyed the comfort of the Holy Spirit. After Paul's conversion, " . . . the churches throughout all Judea, Galilee, and Samaria had peace and were edified. And walking in the fear of the Lord and in the comfort of the Holy Spirit, they were multiplied" (Acts 9:31, NKJV).

This aspect of the Holy Spirit was made very clear to me when my mother passed away. She had a heart attack and a stroke and slipped into a coma while my family was in Colombia. We returned to the United States for three weeks to be with the rest of my family while she was in the hospital. We prayed intensely for her recovery. One night while Cherie sat in the hospital at the bedside of my mother, a figure, whom Cherie recognized as Jesus, stood at the end of the bed and instructed her to just praise the Lord. And then He disappeared. A few days later, my comatose mother was put in a rest home. Though we had to return to Colombia, we tried to consistently obey this message of praising the Lord in spite of the circumstances.

While in Colombia, we kept almost daily contact with family members about my mother. When we finally returned home, I went to stay close by her for a week. There was no improvement in her condition. About two months later we were staying with some friends for whom we were conducting an evangelistic meeting in a town close to where my mother was kept in the rest home. I received a phone call about 1:30 a.m. from my father-in-law and he told me that my mother was in heaven.

Naturally, I was devastated by the news. The Lord had used me to win my mother to the Lord many years previously. She was not only a wonderful mother who had raised six children without the benefit of a husband (our dad was killed in a traffic accident when I was only three) she was also a praying mother, a friend and confidant. I would sorely miss her. The first thing I did was fall on my knees and immediately the Comforter came. I spoke in tongues for 1 1/2 hours and felt the sweet presence of Christ strengthening me. This kind of power source is readily available to all in the time of need.

Notice another benefit of *glossolalia*: *speaking in tongues can bring deliverance*. Jesus taught his disciples, "Now when they bring you to the synagogues and magistrates and authorities, do not worry about how or what you should answer, or what you should say. For the Holy Spirit will teach you in the very hour what you ought to say" (Lk. 12:11–12, NKJV).

The parallel text in Mark's Gospel is very similar. "But when they arrest you and deliver you up, do not worry beforehand, or premeditate what you will speak. But whatever is given you in that hour, speak that: for it is not you who speak, but the Holy Spirit" (Mk. 13:11, NKJV). Obviously, the Holy Spirit can give anointed words spoken with our own vocabulary and in our language that will help bring us deliverance. But there are occasions in which he gives another language for the same purpose.

One of the most notable examples happened in 1922 in the life of H. B. Garlock, an Assemblies of God missionary to Liberia. Garlock went to rescue an African brother, Kuso, from the Pahn, a cannibalistic tribe, going boldly to the hut where the brother was held captive. He cut the frightened and beaten brother loose, and he and Kuso were joined in front of the tent by some other African men who had accompanied Garlock. At this point the villagers came running, many of them carrying spears, and they surrounded Garlock's party. Though Garlock could only understand snatches of the conversation based on other African languages he knew, he realized that the cannibals planned to kill all of them and eat them. The witchdoctor, using a grass wand, went through a long tirade until finally, he laid the wand at Garlock's feet, indicating that he could speak. Garlock began to shake and thought it was out of fear at first but then he realized the Spirit of the Lord had come upon him and the words of Mark 13:11 came to his mind.

Garlock declared,

> Now under the anointing of the Spirit, I stood up. I reached down and picked up the witch doctor's wand which he had laid at my feet. I opened my mouth and began by saying, 'Ny lay . . . ' meaning, 'Listen to me.' And then it happened. The Holy Spirit took complete control of my tongue and vocal organs, and there poured from my lips a torrent of words that I had never learned. I did not know what I said, nor how long I spoke. But when I had finished, silence reigned.[14]

The Holy Spirit had given words that changed the entire scene. The witchdoctor commanded that

a white rooster be brought and sacrificed as a sub-
stitute for the white man and his companions. The
warlike tribe could not do enough for Garlock and
his men after that as they gave them food and helped
carry the wounded man back to safety. Many years
later Garlock reported, "I am happy to say that there
are Spirit-filled pastors and churches throughout the
tribe."[15]

I have heard and read many stories similar to
the one just related.[16] But I have never heard of a
non-Pentecostal who began to speak in a foreign language in an emergency situation or in a time in which
such miraculous intervention was needed!

Still another reason for being filled with the
Spirit is that *boldness follows the infilling of the
Spirit.* Just a glimpse at the lives of the disciples after
Pentecost helps confirm this. Notice an example in
which the disciples specifically prayed for boldness
in Acts 4:23–30. God answered their prayer in dramatic fashion. "And when they had prayed, the place
where they were assembled together was shaken;
and they were all filled with the Holy Spirit, and they
spoke the word of God with boldness" (Acts 4:31,
NKJV). The Holy Spirit produced the boldness that
the disciples needed to speak for Christ in the face of

great persecution.

Finally, *being filled with the Holy Spirit helps the believer in the time of death*. This is seen in Luke's account of Stephen immediately prior to his martyrdom. "But he, being full of the Holy Spirit, gazed into heaven and saw the glory of God and Jesus standing at the right hand of God. And said, 'Look! I see the heavens opened and the Son of Man standing at the right hand of God!'" (Acts 7:54–55, NKJV). When the Spirit of God came over him, Stephen witnessed the glory of God and saw the Lord ready to receive him. As his murderers began throwing stones at him, he made two last requests prior to his death: (1) that the Lord would receive his spirit and (2) that the Lord would not charge his assassins with sin. He was in touch with another world, empowered by the Holy Spirit.

I contend that death is not the enemy of the child of God. I am aware that 1 Cor. 15:26 declares, "The last enemy that will be destroyed is death." (NKJV) But, contextually, Paul is teaching about the death and future resurrection of the saints. Death is an enemy in that those who have died are still dead as far as their physical body is concerned. One day that last enemy, the enemy who has brought decay to the physical body, will be destroyed. The grip of death cannot perpetually keep the body of the saints in total inactivity. Christ will eventually loose the hold of death on His saints (1 Cor. 15:20–28).

In the same fifteenth chapter of First Corinthians, Paul says, "The sting of death is sin" (1 Cor. 15:56, NKJV). The presence of sin produces a sting when death comes. But for the Christian, no sin means no sting. The point is, death does not have to be feared as an evil, lurking foe, personified to the point of being equivalent to Satan or satanic forces. While death may be a horrible experience for the sinner, it is the natural passing of saints into the glorious presence of Christ (Psa. 116:15). It is normal and natural for a human being to instinctively fear death. Inherently, God endowed mankind with strong self-preservation tendencies. But the Holy Spirit can reverse the natural anxieties associated with death and use the occasion for God's glory.

A close personal friend of mine, Pastor L. H. Hubbard of Tyler, Texas, witnessed the victorious homegoing of his father one Sunday morning in 1965. Before preaching, Pastor Hubbard felt that someone might have something to share with the congregation and extended an opportunity for anyone in the audience to speak. His father stood and began quoting scripture that pertained to heaven and the coming of the Lord. When he finished, he sat down and began speaking in tongues. Then, he quietly slumped over in the pew and by the time Pastor Hubbard got to him, his father had gone to be with Jesus. The Holy Spirit gracefully ushered him into the presence of Christ.

The Holy Spirit often uses the Christian's homegoing to lead others to Christ. This happened in dramatic fashion in Vietnam, according to the testimony of Sergeant John McElhannon. Sergeant McElhannon, a Native American Navajo, knew his friend, George, was a Christian because of the life he lived. When George was shot by the Vietcong, John rushed to his side but in a few moments George was gone. However, before he died, George spoke in tongues and said in John's native Navajo language, "John, you need God." John could not forget those words and when he also was wounded and was taken back to the states, he determined to know George's God. After his recuperation, John was directed by the Holy Spirit to an Assemblies of God church where he learned about the power that enabled George to speak his language. John was saved due to the last words that the Holy Spirit enabled a dying Christian to speak.[17]

Chapter Nine

Evidences of Pentecost

This book has primarily focused on the initial, physical evidence of the presence of the Holy Spirit: speaking in tongues. Certainly the initial, or first, evidence has extreme importance. One should start with the essentials.

But a variety of items associated with Pentecost and the Pentecostal experience should be present among believers and evidenced in the local church. Acts 2:42–47 details a number of activities, attitudes and responses of the people after they received the Holy Spirit Baptism.

First, *they exhibited unwavering adherence to the apostles' doctrine* (v. 42). The apostles had walked and talked with the Master for approximately 3 1/2 years. They taught what they knew - the principles, precepts and beliefs that Christ had taught them. Far from being "unlearned and ignorant men" (Acts 4:13) as their accusers claimed, they had been trained by the greatest Teacher of all time. The manner in which they learned from Him before the ascension continued afterwards through the instruction of the Holy Spirit. Jesus spoke of the Holy Spirit to His disciples, declaring, "He will teach you all things" (Jn. 14:26, NKJV) and, "He will guide you into all truth" (Jn. 16:13, NKJV). One can be assured that the doctrine received by the early church was not some fad or "pop" doctrine that would soon be forgotten when some other spectacular "revelation" gained prominence. The early believers had roots grounded in good doctrine.

Second, *the first Pentecostals believed in and practiced close-knit fellowship* (v. 42). Unfortunately, this kind of togetherness is often missing from many congregations today. The early church built a powerful bond that sustained them through difficult times. They enjoyed one another's company and developed close relationships as they came together to worship Christ.

Third, *the first Pentecostal church broke bread together* (v. 42). This verse probably referred to the simple act of participating in a common meal rather than Holy Communion. However, early evidence seems to indicate that the Communion service commemorating the Lord's death grew out of these common meals. By the time Paul advised those hungry among the Corinthians to first eat at home before partaking of the Lord's supper (1 Cor. 11:33–34), he evidently sought to separate the common meal from the practice of Holy Communion.[18]

The fact of Christ's death, burial and resurrection permeated the thoughts, conversation and preaching of the early Church (Acts 2:23–24, 30–33; 3:13–15, 26; 4:2, 10, 33; 5:30–32). It was to be expected that the times of breaking bread together would remind the disciples of the last supper with Christ. His admonition to them to "do this in remembrance of me" (Lk. 22:19, NKJV) would not have soon been forgotten.

The Church today must remember Christ's redemption and victorious resurrection. Holy Communion must be celebrated frequently and must never become commonplace. Without the Calvary event, Pentecost would never have occurred. A true Pentecostal experience drives the individual to focus on Christ and the redemptive process.

Another evidence of true Pentecost is *prayer* (v. 42). The early church met together for prayer, consistently and often. They expected to pray each time they assembled. Their fellowship always involved prayer. A true Pentecostal experience today will be evidenced by the same kind of desire to pray.

Many biblical injunctions support the necessity to pray in all circumstances (Lk. 18:1; Rom. 12:12; Eph. 6:18; Phil. 4:6; 1 Thess. 5:17; I Tim. 2:8; 1 Thess. 5:17; etc.). The following list, though not exhaustive, vividly illustrates the many different facets of effective prayer.

1. Pray in the Holy Spirit—Rom. 8:26–27
2. Pray with the understanding—1 Cor. 14:15
3. Pray fervent prayers—James 5:16
4. Pray believing prayers—Mark 11:24
5. Pray for extended periods—Lk. 6:12
   (Christ, our example, prayed all night)
6. Pray in harmony with God's Word—John 15:7
7. Pray to the Father—Jn. 16:23
8. Pray in Jesus' name—Jn. 14:12–15
9. Pray continually—1 Thess. 5:17
10. Pray, praising God for the Answer—Phil. 4:6

Another noteworthy item seen in those early Pentecostal gatherings entailed *a holy and healthy respect for Almighty God* ("then fear came upon every soul," Acts 2: 43, NKJV). Much can be determined about a person's spiritual walk by the reverence expressed toward his Lord. An intimate relationship with God is evidenced by an individual's respect for Him as a Holy being. The early church saw God's mighty power at Pentecost. The God they served deserved their total allegiance and respect.

A sixth expression of a true Pentecostal experience seen in this context is *continuing evidence of the miraculous demonstrated through Christ's followers.* Luke declared that "many wonders and signs were done through the apostles" (v. 43, NKJV). Without question, mighty miracles of healing have attracted far more attention than the phenomena of speaking in tongues. This was true in the early church and it was true in the early beginnings of Pentecost in this century.

Charles Parham, the earliest proponent in modern times of speaking in tongues as the "sign" or evidence of one's being filled with the Spirit, did not find widespread acceptance of the Pentecostal doctrine until he emphasized divine healing and many individuals were healed.[19] The demonstration of the miraculous corroborated speaking in tongues, as well as soul winning and evangelism. This pattern can be seen in the book of Acts. For example, Peter and John found little resistance for the infilling of the Spirit among the Samaritans since they had already witnessed the miraculous (Acts 8:4–8; 14–17). A Pentecostal church of any generation will inevitably see many signs and wonders.

A seventh characteristic of Pentecost seen in this passage is *unity among believers*. This unity can be noted both in verse 44 and verse 46: "All that believed were together and had all things common" Acts 2:44, KJV; "And they, continuing daily with one accord. . . ." Acts 2:46, KJV. A vibrant experience in the Holy Spirit directs a believer's attention away from perceived differences in the body of believers to a focus on Christ. The early church showed their solidarity not only in word but in deed as well.

An eighth demonstration of a Pentecostal experience is *complete trust in God for His provision* (v. 45, they "sold their possessions and goods," NKJV). It is not always easy to part with valued material possessions, but those first Pentecostal believers relinquished their right of ownership as they fervently obeyed the resurrected Lord. This attitude should prevail in the church today.

Another expression of Pentecost seen in this passage is that *early believers shared with others* (v.

45). They willingly divided their goods among those who had need. A complete lack of selfishness and attachment to material things punctuated their worship.

Notice also, *they faithfully gathered in the temple* (v. 46). The temple still held a very important place in their lives. They thought of the temple as God's dwelling place. They wanted to be in this symbolic expression of the presence of God. A time would come when this temple would be destroyed. But even had it remained, the Christians would not have been welcome because of their insistence on believing in Christ. However, in the infancy of the church, the temple played a very significant role in their worship.

This love for the house of God should still identify Spirit-filled believers today. They should not need to be cajoled, implored, or admonished to attend church. Faithful attendance in a local church, a physical expression of the presence of God, should be a common practice of Spirit-filled believers.

Next, take note that *the early believers practiced their faith consistently and not haphazardly* (v. 46 - *daily*). A constant search after God revealed a true hunger for spiritual things. They went daily to the temple for it represented an opportunity to seek after God. This same desire for daily contact with God resulting in spiritual growth should characterize each individual Christian today.

The twelfth item seen in these verses is that *they nurtured one another in the faith* (v. 46). The early believers went to each other's houses to break bread together. This simple action of coming together in one another's homes was a great source of strength to those early believers. They encouraged one another and grew in faith together. The weak became strong through the constant contact with other believers. These times of nurturing became known as "love feasts." The meal was incidental to the real purpose of praising the Lord together. Luke declares, "They ate their food with gladness and simplicity of heart, praising God . . ." (vs. 46–47, NKJV).

An important part of the nurturing process in these early meetings was that elitism did not appear to permeate their activities. The believers broke bread "from house to house" (Acts 2:46, NKJV) without consideration of status. Priests later on joined their fellowship (Acts 6:7) and eventually their chief per-secutor, Saul of Tarsus, would become one of their staunchest allies. Samaritans and Gentiles would also become members of the body of believers. Social and racial prejudices could not coexist with true Christianity then, and neither is it acceptable now. True Pentecost is evidenced by the ease with which believers accept others into their group and are willing to invite them into their inner circles.

Next, note this evidence of Pentecost among the early believers: *they were people of praise* (v. 47). Praising God occurred naturally when they came together. God had blessed them too much for them to remain silent. They consistently expressed their gratitude to Him for all He had done for them. True Pentecostal believers are still infected with a desire to praise God. Praising God is a natural tendency for those who have been filled with the Holy Spirit.

The fourteenth feature of Pentecostal believers, found in this passage, is that *they were people of character who earned the respect of everyone around them* (v. 47). Without a consistent walk with the Lord, this kind of respect cannot be earned. The early Christians had "favor with all the people" (v. 47, NKJV) because their testimony was not clouded by inconsistency. Pentecostal believers must exhibit quality of character that convinces the world not only of their sincerity but also of their moral rectitude.

Finally, *Pentecost can be evidenced by church growth*. Luke declared, "And the Lord added to the church daily those who were being saved" (Acts 2:47, NKJV). Planning strategies to effect church growth are certainly commendable, but the greatest influence for dynamic growth is a mighty move of the Spirit of God within the church body.

Chapter Ten

Frequently Asked Questions About Speaking in Tongues

Tongues of Angels

In one seminar I conducted on the Baptism in the Holy Spirit, I stated that the Scripture indicates that those who speak in tongues speak in languages known to man. Some older translations of the Bible supply the word "unknown" in front of tongues but that italicized term is not found in older, more reliable manuscripts. After the seminar, one individual asked me, "Do not some speak in the tongues of angels?" The question was based on Paul's statement in First Corinthians 13:1, "Though I speak with the tongues of men and of angels, and have not charity (love), I am become as sounding brass or a tinkling cymbal" (KJV). But Paul was not stating that he spoke in tongues of angels. He was merely saying, "Even if I could speak with the tongues of angels, if I don't have love, I am nothing." There is no indication in the Scripture that the one who speaks in tongues is actually speaking in the tongues of angels.

Speaking in Tongues When Asked to Do So

Should the baptized believer speak in tongues just because someone asks him to do so? Some Pentecostal/Charismatics believe and practice speaking in tongues whenever they decide to or whenever someone asks them to. While it would be impossible for me or anyone else to judge the individual who immediately begins to speak in tongues just because they are requested to do so, there are reasons I am hesitant to endorse this practice.

I certainly feel that one can live so close to God that the presence of the Holy Spirit is very near at all times. However, I feel that God is to be held in awe and reverence also. I would never speak in tongues for someone just so he/she could see how it sounds. Neither would I speak in tongues just because a moderator or director of the service requested that I do so, though I would seek to allow the Spirit to begin to move upon me. I certainly do not want to be a hindrance to the move of the Spirit that the minister or program director is trying to promote.

It is important to maintain a holy reverence for God and the Holy Spirit and not let the experience (of speaking in tongues) ever become anything less than the powerful, miraculous encounter that it is. After all, the Bible plainly says, "And they were all filled with the Holy Ghost, and began to speak with other tongues, as the Spirit gave them utterance" (Acts 2:4, NKJV). It is the Spirit who moves upon us, and then we speak.

Can Unholy People Speak in Tongues?

There have been instances of individuals who did not live holy lives who came to church and spoke in tongues. One individual who had once been in church but did not attend anymore boasted that he could speak in tongues whenever he wished. How is this possible?

When God baptizes us with the Holy Spirit, He gives us a new language. That language pattern is established in the mind just as any other language we may have learned. All speaking must first come through the mind (the brain). It is my opinion that when an unholy person speaks in tongues, he or she is only mouthing words that were once uttered when the Spirit moved powerfully upon them. They still remember those words and are able to recite them. But this is far removed from the sweet presence of the Holy Spirit and the anointing of God's presence. It is dangerous to proceed with such an unhealthy respect for the Holy Spirit.

This is a further reason why I am careful about this wonderful gift in my own life. I never want it to become mechanical or out of my own mind or spirit. I want it to be as precious and as real as it has been from the time I first received the Baptism in the Spirit.

Are You Sure That Everyone Will Speak in Tongues?

In one of my classes about the Holy Spirit, someone cited a good Christian whom they had known who never spoke in tongues. The individual stated that the person was a model Christian but just was unable to receive the Holy Spirit Baptism. The questioner then proceeded to say that perhaps it wasn't God's will to fill that individual.

This has already been discussed in this book. But it brings up a very important issue. We must never allow theology to be determined by our experience. Theology and doctrine can only be decided by the ultimate authority found in the Bible. Anything else is extra-biblical and therefore erroneous.

Keep encouraging individuals to be filled with the Sprit. Even those who have sought for many years can be filled. God has not made an exception in their case.

Is There a Transference of Anointing?

In this day of the outpouring of the Holy Spirit, we have to be careful how we express biblical truth. There are those who feel they must go to certain ministers and/or ministries to be prayed for before they can be used by God. They may already be filled with the Spirit but they haven't had some special blessing by someone being used by the Spirit.

Undeniably, God does use certain individuals in His work to bring about powerful results. I have mentioned in this book the importance of laying on of hands. It is scripturally correct and expected that believers will lay hands on people (Mk. 16:18, 2 Tim. 1:6). When we do, God has promised to visit the recipient of our prayers. The power of God may come upon that individual and he/she may never be the same as a result. In fact, a greater anointing may rest upon that person. However, the way God visits an individual after hands are laid upon him/her is strictly God's business. Furthermore, the laying on of hands is no guarantee of future success. In fact, the Scripture cautions against laying on of hands in recognition of someone's future ministry if the individual receiving the laying on of hands is a novice (1 Tim. 5:22).

Earlier in this book, I used a phrase, "commissioning or transferring of power," referring to some Old Testament passages, particularly one concerning Joshua. This was and is entirely different to the emphasis placed on the value given to the term, "transference of anointing," that is in vogue today. In the illustration used of Moses and Joshua, the laying on of hands signified the future leadership of Joshua.

I do believe that the power of God upon an individual can be felt by others. Perhaps a better terminology would be a "connection of power." But even at that, we must be careful not to assume that only certain individuals or ministries have this divine connection.

There was a time in Church history in which certain individuals began to feel there had to be an apostolic succession in the form of one individual in order for there to be an anointed one to lead his generation. This is a dangerous mindset. The Old Testament does lend itself to a leader laying hands upon his successor as seen in the Old Testament, particularly with the anointing of kings. However, the New Testament teaches the priesthood of all believers (1 Pet. 2:9; Rev. 1:6). Conversion allows us to be mightily used of God, not on the basis of who we are but on the basis of the cross.

To avoid confusion, I feel it is best not to use the term "transference of anointing." We do not want to imply anything which can be interpreted according to some individual's particular bias. I readily understand that we cannot always avoid using nomenclature which will be misinterpreted. But language is important and we need to clarify our intentions when we do use terminology that is suspect.

About the Author

Doyle Jones has served as pastor, educator, and missionary, but he is best known as an evangelist whose ministry has taken him to most of Latin America and to many other areas of the world. Influenced by the late Missionary/Evangelist Richard Jeffrey and others, he dedicated his missionary efforts to establishing churches through an evangelistic ministry which emphasized the miraculous.

Dr. Jones received his Bachelor of Arts from Southwestern Assemblies of God University (SAGU), Waxahachie, Texas. He later earned a Master of Divinity from Assemblies of God Theological Seminary, Springfield, Missouri and completed his Doctor of Ministry at Oral Roberts University, Tulsa, Oklahoma. In 1991, Dr. Jones returned to SAGU to become the Director of Missions for his alma mater, a position he held for fourteen years.

While at SAGU, Jones sought to directly involve his students in street evangelism, church planting, discipleship and other pragmatic approaches which helped to permanently influence the bearer of the message as well as the respondent. Each summer he selected a group of students to accompany him to some foreign country and established fourteen churches while at Southwestern.

Dr. Jones is absolutely convinced of the necessity of being filled with the Spirit. He cites biblical mandates as well as the spiritual dividends reaped by the Spirit-filled believer as important reasons to "be filled with the Spirit." He has personally witnessed hundreds of people experience the *glossalalia* phenomenon in his meetings. This book is a direct result of his many years of evangelistic ministry in which scores of individuals, including persons from may different denominational and theological backgrounds, received the powerful infilling of the Holy Spirit.

Jones is married to Cherie, the daughter of former Assemblies of God pastors, Reverend and Mrs. Lonnie Fogger (both deceased). The Jones' have two sons, Donovan and Nathan, who are pursuing careers in the ministry. Currently, Dr. Jones is involved in writing and speaking and is in demand in the United States and abroad.

For more information or to order
more books please contact:

Doyle Jones
P. O. Box 182
Waxahachie, TX 75168

You can email Doyle at   cherieljones@sbcglobal.net

ENDNOTES

[1] For example, see Stanley M. Horton, *What the Bible Says About the Holy Spirit*, (Springfield, MO: Gospel Publishing House, 1976); Howard M. Ervin, *Spirit Baptism* (Peabody, MA: Hendrickson Publishers, 1987) and B. C. Aker, "Initial Evidence, A Biblical Perspective," *Dictionary of Pentecostal and Charismatic Movements*, eds. Stanley M. Burgess and Gary B. McGee (Grand Rapids: Zondervan Publishing House, 1988), pp. 455–459.

[2] See Leviticus 23:15–21, Exodus 23:16, and Numbers 28:26 in the Old Testament when this festival is known by the following names: "The Feast of Weeks," "The Feast of Ingathering," and "The Day of the Firstfruits." Pentecost means "fifty" in Greek and refers to the Old Testament festival which falls fifty days or seven weeks after the passover.

[3] Stanley M. Horton, *The Book of Acts* (Springfield, MO: Gospel Publishing House, 1994), p. 221.

[4] Horton, *The Book of Acts*, p. 106.

[5] Horton, What the Bible Says About the Holy Spirit, p. 161.

[6] See Psalms 1, 37, 38, and especially Proverbs 11–15.

[7] Horton, *What the Bible Says About the Holy Spirit*, p. 244.

[8] See chapter five.

[9] D. A. Reed, "Oneness Pentecostalism," in *Dictionary of Pentecostal and Charismatic Movements*, pp. 650–651.

[10] Peter Wagner cited in H. V. Synan, *The Spirit Said Grow* (Monrovia, CA: MARC, 1992), pp. i-ii.

[11] Personal interview with Vinson Synan, February 4, 2005. See also Vinson Synan, *The Century of the Holy Spirit* (Nashville: Thomas Nelson Publishers, 2001), p. 372. Synan has documented that the Pentecostal/Charismatics have grown from 530,000,000 to the most recent number, 625,000,000, in just five years.

[12] Donald Gee, *The Fruit of the Spirit*, (Springfield, Missouri: Gospel Publishing House, 1928), p. 15.

[13] W. Robert Cook, *The Theology of John* (Chicago: Moody Press, 1979), p. 122.

[14] H. B. Garlock, *Before We Kill and Eat You* (Dallas, TX: Christ for the Nations, 1974), p. 100.

[15] Garlock, p. 101.

[16] See Ralph W. Harris, *Spoken By the Spirit* (Springfield, MO: Gospel Publishing House, 1973) pp. 1–128; also, John Sherril, *They Speak With Other Tongues* (Grand Rapids: Baker Book House, 1964), pp. 85–115.

[17] Harris, pp. 80–82.

[18] Dennis C. Duling and Norman Perrin, *The New Testament: Proclamation and Parenesis, Myth and History*, 3rd. edition, (Ft. Worth, TX: Harcourt Brace College Publishers, 1994), p. 146.

[19] Paul Chappell, "Great Things He Hath Done: Origins of the Divine Healing Movement in America" (Ph.D., diss.,), p. 221.

Selected Bibliography
and Related Material

Aker, B.C. "Initial Evidence, A Biblical Perspective," pp. 455- 459. *Dictionary of Pentecostal and Charismatic Movements.* Eds. Stanley M. Burgess and Gary B. McGee. Grand Rapids: Zondervan Publishing House, 1988.

Chappell, Paul. "Great Things He Hath Done: Origins of the Divine Healing Movement in America" Ph.D., diss. n.d.

Cook, W. Robert. *The Theology of John.* Chicago: Moody Press, 1979.

Duling, Dennis C. and Norman Perrin, *The New Testament: Proclamation and Parenesis, Myth and History.* 3rd. edition. Ft. Worth, TX: Harcourt Brace College Publishers, 1994.

Ervin, Howard M. *Spirit Baptism.* Peabody, MA: Hendrickson Publishers, 1987.

Garlock, H. B. *Before We Kill and Eat You*. Dallas, TX: Christ for the Nations, 1974.

Gee, Donald. *The Fruit of the Spirit*. Springfield, Missouri: Gospel Publishing House, 1928.

Harris, Ralph W. *Spoken By the Spirit*. Springfield, MO: Gospel Publishing House, 1973.

Holdcroft, L. Thomas. *The Holy Spirit, A Pentecostal Interpretation*. Revised Edition. Abbotsford, Canada: CeeTeC Publishing, 1999.

Horton, Stanley M. *The Book of Acts*. Springfield, MO: Gospel Publishing House, 1994.

Horton, Stanley M. *What the Bible Says About the Holy Spirit*. Springfield, MO: Gospel Publishing House, 1976.

Palma, Anthony D. *The Holy Spirit, A Pentecostal Perspective*. Springfield, MO: Gospel Publishing House, 2001.

Rea, John. *Bible Handbook on the Holy Spirit*. Orlando, FL: 1998.

Reed, D. A. "Oneness Pentecostalism," pp. 650–651. in *Dictionary of Pentecostal and Charismatic Movements*, Eds. Stanley M. Burgess and Gary B. McGee. Grand Rapids: Zondervan Publishing House, 1988.

Sherril, John. *They Speak With Other Tongues*. Grand Rapids: Baker Book House, 1964.

Stronstad, Roger. *The Charismatic Theology of Luke*. Peabody, MA: Hendrickson, 1984.

Synan, Vinson. Personal Interview (February 4, 2005).

Synan, Vinson. *The Century of the Holy Spirit*. Nashville: Thomas Nelson Publishers, 2001.

Wagner, Peter. Cited in H. V. Synan. *The Spirit Said Grow*. Monrovia, CA: MARC, 1992.

Warner, Wayne, Ed. *Touched By The Fire*. Plainfield, NJ: Logos International, 1978.

Contact Doyle Jones at
cherieljones@sbcglobal.net
www.doylejonesministries.org
or order more copies of this book at

TATE PUBLISHING, LLC

127 East Trade Center Terrace
Mustang, Oklahoma 73064

(888) 361 - 9473

Tate Publishing, LLC

www.tatepublishing.com